TINY STORIES FOR GERMAN LEARNERS

Short Stories in German for Beginners and Intermediate Learners

Hans Fischer

This book was designed using resources from www.freepik.com

greenthumbpublishing@gmail.com

Contents

Introduction

Reading in a foreign language is one of the most effective ways for you to improve language skills and expand vocabulary. However, it can sometimes be difficult to find engaging reading materials at an appropriate level that provide a feeling of achievement and a sense of progress. Most books and articles written for native speakers can be too long and difficult to understand or may have very high-level vocabulary so you feel overwhelmed and give up. If these problems sound familiar, then this book is for you!

Tiny Stories for German learners is a collection of 25 unconventional and entertaining short stories that are designed to help beginner to intermediate level German learners improve their language skills.

These short stories create a supportive reading environment by including;

- Rich linguistic content in different genres to keep you entertained and expose you to a variety of word forms.
- Shorter stories in chapters to give you the satisfaction of finishing stories and progressing quickly.
- Texts written at your level so they are more easily comprehended and not overwhelming.
- English translation on alternating pages so you can directly refer to it line by line while reading the German story.
- Key vocabulary is printed **bold** throughout the story and translation to help you understand unfamiliar words more easily.
- Comprehension questions to test your understanding of key events and to encourage you to read in more

detail.

So whether you want to expand your vocabulary, improve your comprehension, or simply read for fun, this book is the biggest step forward you will take in your studies this year. Tiny stories for German learners will give you all the support you need, so sit back, relax, and let your imagination run wild as you are transported to a magical world of adventure, mystery and intrigue – in German!

How to use this book

Reading is a difficult talent to master. We use a range of micro-skills to help us read in our native languages. For example, we might skim a passage to get a rough understanding, or gist, of what it's about. Alternatively, we might comb through numerous pages of a train schedule in search of a specific time or location. While these micro-skills are second nature when reading in our native languages, research reveals that we often forget most of them when reading in a foreign language. When learning a foreign language, we normally begin at the beginning of a text and work our way through it, trying to understand every single word. Inevitably, we come across unfamiliar or complex terms and become annoyed by our inability to comprehend them.

One of the biggest advantages of reading in a foreign language is that you are exposed to a vast number of phrases and expressions that are used in everyday situations. Extensive reading is a term used to describe reading for pleasure in order to learn a language. It's not like reading a textbook, when conversations or texts are designed to be read slowly and carefully with the goal of comprehending every word. "Intensive reading" refers to reading that is done to achieve specific learning goals or complete tasks. To put it another way, thorough reading in textbooks usually aids in the learning of grammar rules and particular vocabulary, but extensive reading of stories aids in the learning of natural language.

Tiny stories for German learners will provide you with opportunities to learn more about natural German

language in use, although you may have started your language learning journey with solely textbooks. Here are a few pointers to keep in mind as you read the stories in this book to get the most out of them: When it comes to reading, enjoyment and a sense of accomplishment are critical. You keep coming back for more because you enjoy what you're reading. Reading each story from beginning to end is the best method to enjoy reading stories and feel accomplished. As a result, the most crucial thing is to get to the end of a story. It's actually more crucial than knowing every single word

The more you read, the more you will gain knowledge. You will quickly have a knowledge of how German works if you read larger books for pleasure. However, keep in mind that in order to get the full benefits of extensive reading, you must first read a sufficiently substantial volume. Reading a few pages here and there may teach you a few new words, but it won't make a significant difference in your overall level of German.

Accept the fact that you will not comprehend everything you read in a novel. This is, without a doubt, the most crucial point! Always remember that not understanding all of the words or sentences is entirely acceptable. It does not imply that your language skills are inadequate or that you are performing poorly. It indicates that you are actively involved in the learning process.

Reading guide

In order to get the most from reading Tiny Stories for German Learners, it will be best for you to follow this simple six-step reading process for each chapter of the stories:

1. Read the chapter title. Think about what the story might be about. Then read the story all the way through. Your aim is simply to reach the end of the story. Therefore, do not stop to look up words and do not worry if there are things you do not understand. Simply try to follow the plot.

2. When you reach the end of the story, scan the English translation to see if you have understood what has happened and pick up any context you may have missed.

3. Go back and read the same story again. If you like, you can focus more on story details than before, but otherwise simply read it through one more time.

4. Next, work through the comprehension questions in German to check your understanding of key events in the story. If you do not understand the questions fully, do not worry. Use you knowledge to answer as best you can.

5. At this point, you should have some understanding of the main events of the chapter. If not, you may wish to re-read the chapter a few times using the translation to check unknown words and phrases until you feel confident.

Once you are ready and confident that you understand what has happened – whether it's after one reading of the story or several – move on to the next story and continue

enjoying the story at your own pace, just as you would any other book.

Only once you have completed a story in its entirety should you consider going back and studying the story language in more depth if you wish. Or instead of worrying about understanding everything, take time to focus on all that you have understood and congratulate yourself for all that you have done.

TINY STORIES

FOR GERMAN LEARNERS

Street Food probieren

Das erste Mal, dass ich deutsches Streetfood gegessen habe, war während einer Reise nach Berlin. Ich **erinnere mich, dass ich** eine gefühlte Ewigkeit in der Schlange stand, aber das war es wert, als ich endlich diese leckere Currywurst in die Finger bekam. Die Wurst war so saftig und die Currysauce war perfekt. Auch die knusprigen Pommes frites, die es dazu gab, fand ich klasse. Es war eine so einfache Mahlzeit, aber sie hat **fantastisch** geschmeckt. Seitdem bin ich süchtig nach **deutschem** Straßenessen. Wann immer ich in Berlin bin, muss ich mir eine Currywurst und Pommes besorgen (und manchmal sogar eine Brezel oder zwei). Aber auch wenn ich nicht in Deutschland bin, sehne ich mich von Zeit zu Zeit nach diesen Geschmacksrichtungen. Deshalb habe ich mich entschlossen, mein eigenes deutsches Street Food zu Hause zuzubereiten. Es bedurfte einiger Versuche (und einer Menge Essen), aber **schließlich habe** ich meine eigene Version der Currywurst perfektioniert. **Wenn ich** jetzt Lust auf etwas Herzhaftes und Würziges habe, brauche ich nur den Grill anzuwerfen und ein paar Würstchen zuzubereiten! Ich stand in der Schlange vor dem Currywurststand, und mir lief das Wasser im Mund zusammen. Ich konnte den Geruch der gegrillten Würstchen riechen und mein Magen knurrte.

Endlich war ich an der Reihe, zu bestellen. "Eine Currywurst bitte", sagte ich, während ich ein paar Euro

Trying street food

The first time I ever had German **street** food was during a trip to Berlin. I **remember** standing in line for what felt like forever, but it was worth it once I finally got my hands on that delicious currywurst. The sausage was so juicy and the curry sauce was perfect. I also loved the crispy fries that came with it. It was such a simple meal, but it tasted **amazing**. Since then, I've been hooked on **German** street food. Whenever I'm in Berlin, I make sure to get my fix of currywurst and fries (and sometimes even a pretzel or two). But even when I'm not in Germany, I still crave those flavours from time to time. That's why I decided to try making my own German street food at home. It took some trial and error (and a lot of eating), but **eventually** I perfected my own version of currywurst. Now **whenever** I'm craving something hearty and flavorful, all I have to do is fire up the grill and cook up some sausages! I was standing in line at the Currywurst stand, my mouth watering in anticipation. I could smell the sausage grilling and it made my stomach growl.

Finally, it was my turn to order. "One currywurst please," I said as I handed over some Euros. The woman behind the counter smiled and placed a **steaming** hot sausage on a paper plate for me. She then **squirted** some curry sauce over it and added a handful of fries before handing it all over. I took my food and found a spot to sit down at one of the nearby picnic tables. Then I dug in, savouring every bite of that delicious **German** street food. The sausage was juicy and flavorful, while the

übergab. Die Frau hinter dem Tresen lächelte und legte mir eine **dampfend** heiße Wurst auf einen Pappteller. Dann **spritzte** sie etwas Currysauce darüber und gab eine Handvoll Pommes dazu, bevor sie mir das Ganze überreichte. Ich nahm mein Essen und suchte mir einen Platz an einem der nahe gelegenen Picknicktische. Dann stürzte ich mich darauf und genoss jeden Bissen dieses köstlichen **deutschen** Straßenessens. Die Wurst war saftig und würzig, und die Currysauce gab genau die richtige Menge an Schärfe hinzu. Und die knusprigen Pommes frites waren perfekt, um sie in die extra Portion Soße zu tunken! Ich spazierte durch die Straßen Berlins und nahm alle Sehenswürdigkeiten und Geräusche in mich auf. Die Stadt war voller Menschen, und es gab so viele Dinge zu sehen.

Ich kam an einigen **Straßenhändlern vorbei**, die alles von Brezeln bis hin zu **Würstchen** verkauften, aber mein Magen war schon voll vom Mittagessen, also ging ich weiter. Plötzlich duftete es nach Currywurst, und mir lief das Wasser im Mund zusammen. Ich konnte nicht widerstehen, noch einen letzten Snack zu mir zu nehmen, bevor ich mich auf den Weg zu meinem Hotelzimmer machte. Also machte ich mich auf den Weg zum Currywurststand und stellte mich in die Schlange. Ein paar **Minuten** später hatte ich eine leckere Wurst mit Currysauce in der Hand. Ich fand einen freien Platz an einem Picknicktisch in der Nähe und setzte mich hin, um meine Leckerei zu genießen. Die Wurst war saftig und schmackhaft, und das Curry gab ihr genau die richtige Würze. Es war eine so einfache Mahlzeit, aber sie hat fantastisch geschmeckt!

curry sauce added just the right amount of spice. And those crispy fries were perfect for dipping into that extra bit of sauce! I was walking through the streets of Berlin, taking in all the sights and sounds. The city was bustling with people, and there were so many things to see.

I passed by a few street **vendors** selling everything from pretzels to **sausages**, but my stomach was already full from lunch, so I kept walking. Suddenly, the smell of currywurst wafted through the air, and my mouth started watering.I couldn't resist **getting** one last snack before heading back to my hotel room. So I made my way over to the currywurst stand and got in line. A few **minutes** later, I had my hands on a delicious sausage smothered in curry sauce. I found an empty spot at a nearby picnic table and sat down to enjoy my treat. The sausage was juicy and flavorful, while the curry added just the right amount of spice. It was such a simple meal, but it tasted amazing!

Verständnisfragen

1. Was sagt die Autorin über ihre ersten Erfahrungen mit deutschem Streetfood?

2. Was sagt der Autor über die Wurst?

3. Was sagt der Autor über die Currysauce?

4. Was sagt der Autor über die Pommes frites?

5. Was sagt der Autor über das deutsche Straßenessen im Allgemeinen?

6. Was sagt die Autorin über ihre Vorliebe für deutsches Straßenessen?

7. Was sagt der Autor über den Versuch, deutsches Straßenessen zu Hause zuzubereiten?

8. Was sagt die Autorin über das zweite Mal, als sie deutsches Straßenessen gegessen hat?

9. Was sagt der Autor über den Geruch von Currywurst?

Comprehension Questions

1. What does the author say about her first experience with German street food?

2. What does the author say about the sausage?

3. What does the author say about the curry sauce?

4. What does the author say about the fries?

5. What does the author say about German street food in general?

6. What does the author say about her craving for German street food?

7. What does the author say about trying to make German street food at home?

8. What does the author say about the second time she had German street food?

9. What does the author say about the smell of currywurst?

Brandenburger Tor

Das Brandenburger Tor war einst ein Symbol für Hoffnung und Freiheit. Doch jetzt erinnert es an die dunklen Tage der Vergangenheit. Das Tor ist mit Graffiti **beschmiert**, und der Boden rundherum ist mit Müll übersät. Es ist Jahre her, dass jemand diesen Ort besucht hat. Aber heute **ist etwas** ist anders. Eine junge Frau nähert sich dem Tor und zögert einen Moment, bevor sie hindurch tritt. Sie schaut sich die **Trostlosigkeit** und Traurigkeit um, die sie umgibt, und kann sich eines Gefühls der Verzweiflung nicht erwehren. Doch dann sieht sie etwas, das ihren Blick fesselt: eine einzelne Blume, die aus den Rissen im Pflaster wächst. Sie bückt sich, um sie aufzuheben, denn sie spürt, dass sie jemand von der anderen Straßenseite aus beobachtet. Als sie aufblickt, sieht sie einen alten Mann, der sie **aufmerksam anschaut**. Er sagt nichts, aber er nickt leicht mit dem Kopf, als wolle er "Willkommen" sagen. Die Frau lächelt ihm zu, bevor sie sich abwendet und in Richtung Stadtzentrum **geht**. Sie weiß, dass es hier noch Menschen gibt, denen dieser Ort am Herzen liegt; Menschen, die ihn noch nicht aufgegeben haben.

Vielleicht werden andere eines Tages sehen, was sie sieht: dass es auch in der Dunkelheit Schönheit geben kann; dass es auch in der **Traurigkeit** Hoffnung geben kann. Die Frau geht durch die Straßen der Stadt und nimmt die Sehenswürdigkeiten und Geräusche um sich herum in sich auf. Sie war noch nie an diesem Ort,

Brandenburg gate

The Brandenburg Gate was once a symbol of hope and freedom. But now it is a reminder of the dark days of the past. The gate is **covered** with graffiti, and the ground around it is littered with trash. It has been years since anyone has visited this place. But today **something** is different. A young woman approaches the gate and hesitates for a moment before stepping through. She looks around at the **desolation** and sadness that surrounds her and can't help but feel a sense of despair. But then she sees something that catches her eye: a single flower growing from the cracks in the pavement. She bends down to pick it up, sensing that someone is watching her from across the street. When she looks up, she sees an old man looking at her **intently**. He says nothing, but he nods his head slightly, as if to say "welcome." The woman smiles at him before turning away and **walking** toward the center of town. She knows there are still people here who care about this place; people who haven't given up on it yet.

Maybe one day others will see what she sees: that there can be beauty even in the darkness; that there can be hope even in the **sadness**. The woman walks the streets of the city, taking in the sights and sounds around her. She has never been to this place before, but she feels a connection to it. Maybe it's because she knows what it used to be; maybe it's **because** she can see what it could be again. As she **approaches** the center of town, she hears music **coming** from one of the side streets. It is a beautiful melody that fills her with

aber sie fühlt sich mit ihm verbunden. Vielleicht liegt es daran, dass sie weiß, was es einmal war; vielleicht liegt es **daran, dass** sie sehen kann, was es wieder sein könnte. Als sie **sich dem** Stadtzentrum nähert, hört sie Musik aus einer der Seitenstraßen. Es ist eine wunderschöne Melodie, die sie mit Hoffnung erfüllt. Sie folgt dem Klang, bis sie zu einem kleinen Park kommt, in dem ein alter Mann auf seiner Geige für jeden, der zuhören will, spielt. Sie setzt sich auf eine Bank und schließt die Augen, um sich von der Musik berieseln zu lassen. Als er aufhört zu spielen, öffnet sie die Augen, und **um sie herum ertönt** Beifall. Der alte Mann verbeugt sich höflich, packt sein Instrument ein und geht.

Die **Frau** bleibt noch eine Weile im Park und genießt die Ruhe und den Frieden, bevor sie in ihr Hotelzimmer zurückkehrt. Als sie in dieser Nacht einschläft, träumt sie von einer Zeit, in der diese Stadt wieder lebendig ist, in der die Menschen wieder stolz sind, in der ihre Tore für alle offen sind, die nach Freiheit suchen. Die Frau steht wieder am Brandenburger Tor, aber dieses Mal ist sie nicht allein. Menschen aus der ganzen Welt sind gekommen, um dieses einst große **Symbol** der Hoffnung und der Freiheit zu sehen. Das Tor ist **gereinigt** und die Umgebung in einen schönen Park verwandelt worden. Freude und Optimismus liegen in der Luft, und die Frau kann sich des Gefühls nicht erwehren, dass jetzt **alles** möglich ist. Sie weiß, dass diese Stadt ihren Anteil an der Dunkelheit hatte, aber sie weiß auch, dass die Menschen hier stark genug sind, alles zu überwinden.

hope. She follows the sound until she comes to a small park where an old man is playing his violin for anyone who will listen. She sits down on a bench and closes her eyes to let the music wash over her. When he stops playing, she opens her eyes and applause rings out **around** her. The old man bows politely, packs up his instrument and leaves.

The **woman** stays in the park for a while, enjoying the peace and quiet, before **heading** back to her hotel room. As she falls asleep that night, she dreams of a time when this city is alive again, when people are proud once more, when its gates are open to all who seek freedom. The woman stands at the Brandenburg Gate again, but this time she is not alone. People from all over the world have come to see this once great **symbol** of hope and freedom. The gate has been **cleaned** and the surrounding area has been transformed into a beautiful park. Joy and optimism are in the air, and the woman can't help but feel that **anything** is possible now. She knows that this city has had its share of darkness, but she also knows that the people here are strong enough to overcome anything.

Verständnisfragen

1. Wo befindet sich das Brandenburger Tor?

2. Wie sieht das Brandenburger Tor heute aus?

3. Wann wurde das Brandenburger Tor gebaut?

4. Was ist das Brandenburger Tor, das als Symbol dient?

5. Was ist das Brandenburger Tor heute für ein Symbol?

6. Wie viele Tore gibt es am Brandenburger Tor?

7. Wie viele Menschen können durch das Brandenburger Tor gehen?

8. Was ist, wenn man durch das Brandenburger Tor geht?

9. Wie fühlt sich die Frau, als sie das Brandenburger Tor sieht?

Comprehension Questions

1. Where is the Brandenburg Gate?

2. What does the Brandenburg Gate look like today?

3. When was the Brandenburg Gate built?

4. What is the Brandenburg Gate used to be a symbol?

5. What is the Brandenburg Gate a symbol today?

6. How many gates are there in the Brandenburg Gate?

7. How many people can pass through the Brandenburg Gate?

8. What is when you pass through the Brandenburg Gate?

9. How does the woman feel when she sees the Brandenburg Gate?

Biergarten in München

Die Sonne ging über der Stadt München unter, und der **Biergarten füllte sich** langsam mit Menschen. Die Luft war dick mit dem Geruch von Hopfen und Malz, und der Klang von Lachen und **Gesprächen** erfüllte die Luft. Überall im Garten waren Tische aufgestellt, und die Kellner waren damit beschäftigt, Bestellungen aufzunehmen und Getränke **zu servieren**. In einer Ecke spielte eine Band traditionelle **deutsche Musik**, und die Leute tanzten zu den flotten Klängen. Es war ein perfekter Abend, um mit Freunden ein kühles Bier im Freien zu genießen. Und genau das tat Hans Müller jeden Abend nach der Arbeit. Er setzte sich an seinen Lieblingstisch in der Nähe des Musikpavillons, trank ein paar Bier, hörte Musik, plauderte mit alten und neuen Freunden und sah zu, wie Paare um ihn herum im Takt der Musik tanzten. Der heutige Abend schien auf den ersten Blick wie jeder andere Abend zu sein. Doch als Hans sich umsah, **bemerkte er, dass** heute Abend etwas anders war: Es schienen mehr Familien als sonst da zu sein. Die Eltern saßen an den Tischen und unterhielten sich, während ihre **Kinder** herumliefen und Spiele spielten oder sich gegenseitig **von** Tisch zu Tisch jagten. Es dauerte nicht lange, bis Hans war er von lachenden Kindern umgeben, die um ihn herum Fangen spielten.

Er musste über ihre **Unschuld** schmunzeln, denn sie

Beer garden in Munich

The sun was setting over the city of Munich, and the beer **garden** was starting to fill up with people. The air was thick with the smell of hops and malt, and the sound of laughter and **conversation** filled the air. Tables were set up all around the garden, and waiters were busy taking orders and **serving** drinks. There was a band playing traditional **German** music in one corner, and people were dancing along to the lively tunes. It was a perfect evening for enjoying a cold beer outdoors with friends. And that's exactly what Hans Muller did every night after work. He would sit at his **favourite** table near the bandstand, drink a few beers, listen to music, chat with friends old and new, and watch as couples danced around him in time to the music. Tonight seemed like any other night at first glance. But as Hans looked around he **noticed** something different about tonight's crowd; there seemed to be more families than usual. Parents were sitting at tables chatting while their **children** ran around playing games or chasing each other **between** tables. It wasn't long before Hans found himself surrounded by laughing children as they played tag around him.

He couldn't help but smile at their **innocence**; it reminded him of his own childhood growing up in **Munich**. Hans Muller loved his city, and he loved the beer garden. It was a place where people from all

erinnerte ihn an seine eigene Kindheit in **München**. Hans Müller liebte seine Stadt, und er liebte den Biergarten. Es war ein Ort, an dem Menschen aus allen Gesellschaftsschichten zusammenkamen, um sich zu entspannen, Kontakte zu knüpfen und einfach den **Genuss** eines kalten Bieres an einem warmen Abend zu genießen. Er kam schon seit Jahren hierher, seit er alt genug war, um zu trinken. Und in all dieser Zeit hatte er es noch nie so **voll** mit Familien gesehen. Die Kinder, die **zwischen den** Tischen herumliefen, waren voller Energie, ihr Lachen erfüllte die Luft. Sie schienen so viel Spaß zu haben, dass es Hans glücklich machte, ihnen zuzusehen, und er **erinnerte sich daran, wie es** war, so jung und sorglos zu sein. Plötzlich rannte eines der Kinder in ihn hinein und stieß **versehentlich** sein Bierglas um.

Hans schimpfte leicht mit dem Kind, konnte sich aber ein Lachen nicht verkneifen; es weckte **Erinnerungen** an die Zeit, in der er **selbst** solche Dinge getan hatte. Nach einer Weile verspürte Hans wieder Durst, also ging er zur Bar, um sich **ein weiteres** Bier zu holen. Während er auf sein Getränk wartete, bemerkte er eine Gruppe von Kindern, die sich um einen der Tische versammelt hatte. Sie zeigten auf etwas und lachten. Neugierig ging Hans hinüber, um zu sehen, was sie anschauten. Es war ein Baby, das auf dem Boden unter dem Tisch herumkrabbelte. Hans Müller saß an seinem Lieblingstisch in der Nähe des **Musikpavillons,** trank sein Bier und **beobachtete**, wie sich Familien im Münchner Biergarten vergnügten.

walks of life came to relax, socialize, and enjoy the simple **pleasure** of a cold beer on a warm evening. He had been coming here for years, ever since he was old enough to drink. And in all that time he had never seen it so **crowded** with families. The children running around **between** the tables were full of energy, their laughter filling the air. They seemed to be having so much fun; it made Hans happy just to watch them. He **remembered** what it was like to be   young and carefree like that. Suddenly, one of the children ran into him **accidentally** knocking over his beer glass.

Hans scolded the child lightly but couldn't help but laugh as well; it brought back **memories** of when he used to do things like that **himself**. After a while, Hans started to feel thirsty again so he went to the bar to get **another** beer. As he was waiting for his drink, he noticed a group of children gathered around one of the tables. They were pointing at something and laughing. Curious, Hans walked over to see what they were looking at. It was a baby crawling around on the ground under the table. Hans Muller sat at his **favourite** table near **bandstand** drinking his beer and **watching** as families enjoyed themselves in Munich beer garden.

Verständnisfragen

1. Was sagt der Autor über den Geruch in der Luft?

2. Was macht Hans Müller jede Nacht?

3. Was fällt Hans Müller auf, was an der Menge heute Abend anders ist?

4. Woran erinnern die Kinder Hans Müller?

5. Was denkt Hans Müller über die herumlaufenden Kinder?

6. Was macht Hans Muller am liebsten im Biergarten?

7. Was denkt Hans Müller über die Familien im Biergarten?

Comprehension Questions

1. What does the author say about the smell in the air?

2. What does Hans Muller do every night?

3. What does Hans Muller notice that is different about the crowd tonight?

4. What do the children remind Hans Muller of?

5. What does Hans Muller think about the children run ning around?

6. What is Hans Muller's favourite thing to do in the beer garden?

7. What does Hans Muller think about the families in the beer garden?

Weihnachtsmarkt

Es war ein kalter Wintertag, und der Weihnachtsmarkt war in vollem Gange. Die **Stände** waren festlich geschmückt, und die Luft war erfüllt vom Geruch von Glühwein und gerösteten Kastanien. Ich **schlenderte** umher und nahm all die Sehenswürdigkeiten und Geräusche des **Marktes in mich auf**, als ich plötzlich etwas entdeckte, das mein Herz zum Stillstand brachte. Vor mir stand ein Stand, an dem handgefertigtes Holzspielzeug verkauft wurde. Und zwischen all den anderen Spielsachen stach mir eines sofort ins Auge - eine **wunderschöne** kleine Nussknackerpuppe. Ich wusste **sofort,** dass ich sie haben musste. Ich sprach die Verkäuferin an und fragte, wie viel sie kostete. Sie sagte mir, dass sie fünfzig **Dollar** kostete **- mehr** als ich jemals zuvor für ein Spielzeug bezahlt hatte! Aber ich zögerte nicht, übergab das Geld und nahm meinen neuen Schatz in Besitz.

Sobald ich zu Hause war, konnte ich es kaum erwarten, mehr über meine neue Nussknackerpuppe herauszufinden. Soweit ich es von ihrem schlichten Aussehen her beurteilen konnte, schien sie ziemlich alt zu sein... aber wer wusste das schon so genau? Nachdem ich im Internet **recherchiert hatte**, fand ich heraus, dass diese Art von Puppen in Deutschland in den 1800er Jahren sehr beliebt war - was bedeutete, dass mein kleiner **Nussknacker** weit über 200 Jahre alt sein könnte! Wenn ich nur daran denke, fühle ich mich noch mehr mit ihm verbunden.

Christmas Market

It was a cold winter day, and the **Christmas** market was in full swing. The **stalls** were decked out with festive decorations, and the air was filled with the smell of mulled wine and roasted chestnuts. I **wandered** around, taking in all the sights and sounds of the **market**, when I suddenly spotted something that made my heart stop. There in front of me was a stall selling handmade wooden toys. And amongst all the other toys, there was one that caught my eye immediately – a **beautiful** little nutcracker doll. I knew **instantly** that I had to have it. I approached the stallholder and asked how much it was. She told me it was fifty **dollars**–more than I had ever paid for a toy before! But I didn't hesitate; I handed over the money and took possession of my new treasure.

As soon as I got home, I couldn't wait to find out more about my new **nutcracker** doll. So far as I could tell from its simple appearance, it appeared to be quite old... but who knew for sure? After doing some **research** online, I discovered that these types of dolls were actually very popular in Germany during the 1800s—which meant my little **nutcracker** could be well over 200 years old! Just thinking about it made me feel even more attached to him.
Now that I knew a bit more about my new toy, it was time to give him (or her) a name. After much **deliberation**, I decided on "Klaus"—after the **famous** German folk character who brings children presents at Christmas time. It seemed like the perfect fit. Klaus quickly became a cherished member of our family.

Da ich nun etwas mehr über mein neues Spielzeug wusste, war es an der Zeit, ihm (oder ihr) einen Namen zu geben. Nach reiflicher **Überlegung** entschied ich mich für "Klaus" - nach der **berühmten** deutschen Volksfigur, die Kindern zur Weihnachtszeit Geschenke bringt. Das schien perfekt zu passen. Klaus wurde schnell zu einem geschätzten Mitglied unserer Familie. Von da an nahm er jedes Jahr in der Weihnachtszeit einen stolzen Platz auf unserem Kaminsims ein. Und jedes Jahr verbrachte ich einige Zeit damit, mit ihm zu plaudern und ihm alles zu erzählen, was in meinem Leben passiert war, seit wir das letzte Mal miteinander gesprochen hatten. Es mag albern klingen, aber ich hatte das Gefühl, dass er mir wirklich zuhörte und alles verstand, was ich sagte!

Im Laufe der Jahre, als jedes **Weihnachten** kam und ging, wurde **Klaus** mehr als nur eine Puppe für mich... er wurde mein Freund. Dann, ein Jahr später, änderte sich alles. Ich wachte am Weihnachtsmorgen auf und stellte fest, dass Klaus nicht mehr auf dem Kaminsims stand. Zuerst dachte ich, er müsse **über Nacht** heruntergefallen und zerbrochen sein... aber **nirgends war eine** Spur von ihm zu sehen. Danach habe ich Klaus nie wieder gesehen - aber auch wenn er nicht mehr da ist, wird er immer einen **besonderen** Platz in meinem Herzen haben. Wenn ich jetzt den **Weihnachtsmarkt** besuche, nehme ich mir immer einen Moment Zeit, um die Nussknackerpuppen zu betrachten, die dort verkauft werden... und manchmal frage ich mich sogar, ob eine von ihnen mein alter Freund Klaus sein könnte, **der** zurückkommt, um noch einmal Hallo zu sagen.

Every year from then on, he would take pride of place
on our mantelpiece during the festive season. And
every year, I would spend some time chatting with him,
telling him all about what had happened in my life since
we last spoke. It might sound silly, but it felt like he
really was listening and understanding everything I said!

Over the years, as each **Christmas** came and went,
Klaus became more than just a doll to me... he became
my friend. Then, one year later, everything changed. I
woke up on Christmas morning to find that Klaus was
gone from the mantelpiece. At first, I thought he must
have fallen and broken **overnight**... but there was no
sign of him **anywhere**. It was as if he had vanished into
thin air.I never saw Klaus again after that – but even
though he's gone, he'll always hold a **special** place in
my heart. Whenever I visit the **Christmas** market now, I
always take a moment to look at the nutcracker dolls on
sale... and sometimes I even find myself wondering if
one of them might be my old friend Klaus, **coming** back
to say hello once again.

Verständnisfragen

1. Was war die erste Reaktion des Protagonisten, als er die Nussknackerpuppe sah?

2. Wie viel hat der Protagonist für die Nussknackerpuppe bezahlt?

3. Wie hat der Protagonist die Nussknackerpuppe genannt?

4. Wo ist die Nussknackerpuppe hingegangen, als der Protagonist am Weihnachtsmorgen aufgewacht ist?

5. Warum glaubt der Protagonist, dass die Nussknackerpuppe verschwunden ist?

6. Was macht der Protagonist, wenn er jetzt den Weihnachtsmarkt besucht?

7. Welche Nachforschungen hat der Protagonist über die Herkunft der Nussknackerpuppe angestellt?

8. Welche Gefühle hat der Protagonist gegenüber der Nussknackerpuppe?

Comprehension Questions

1. What was the protagonist's initial reaction upon seeing the nutcracker doll?

2. How much did the protagonist pay for the nutcracker doll?

3. What did the protagonist name the nutcracker doll?

4. Where did the nutcracker doll go when the protagonist woke up on Christmas morning?

5. Why does the protagonist think the nutcracker doll vanished?

6. What does the protagonist do when they visit the Christmas market now?

7. What was the protagonist's research about the nutcracker doll's origins?

8. What feeling does the protagonist have towards the nutcracker doll?

Hamburger Hafen

Der Hamburger Hafen ist ein geschäftiger Ort. **Schiffe** aus der ganzen Welt kommen und gehen, und es gibt immer etwas zu sehen. Ich wollte schon immer einmal dorthin und bekam schließlich die Gelegenheit, als meine Freundin mich **einlud**, sie auf einem Ausflug zu begleiten. Wir kamen früh am Morgen an, gerade als die Sonne ging auf. Die Luft war kalt, aber frisch, und der Geruch von Salzwasser war belebend. Wir gingen hinunter zu den Docks, **wo** wir die Schiffe sehen konnten, die in den Hafen ein- und ausliefen. Es gab so viele davon! Und sie waren alle so unterschiedlich - manche klein und schnittig, andere groß und **träge**. Es war erstaunlich, wie präzise sie in ihre Liegeplätze hinein- und herausmanövrierten. Dabei sahen wir ein Schiff einlaufen, das den **bunten** Flaggen an den Masten nach zu urteilen aus Afrika oder vielleicht sogar aus Indien stammen könnte.

Meine Freundin erzählte mir, dass diese Art von Schiff als **Frachter** bezeichnet wird, weil es keine Passagiere, sondern Fracht befördert, wie die meisten anderen Schiffe heutzutage. Sie sagte, dass man manchmal Leute an Deck **arbeiten** sieht, während das Schiff durch den Hafen fährt - könnt ihr euch das vorstellen? Aber heute war niemand **an Bord** zu sehen, außer oben im Krähennest, wo jemand hoch über allem, was unter ihm an Deck passiert, Ausschau hielt. Nachdem wir das Treiben **im Hafen** eine Weile beobachtet hatten,

Hamburg Harbor

The harbour of Hamburg is a bustling place. **Ships** from all over the world come and go, and there is always something to see. I had always wanted to visit, and finally got my chance when my friend **invited** me to join her on a trip. We **arrived** early in the morning, just as the sun was rising. The air was cold but fresh, and the smell of salt water was invigorating. We walked down to the docks, **where** we could see the ships coming in and out of the harbor. There were so many of them! And they were all so different—some small and sleek, others large and **sluggish** looking. It was amazing to watch them **manoeuvre** in and out of their berths with such precision. As we watched, we saw a ship coming in that looked like it might be from Africa or maybe even India, judging by its **colourful** flags flying from its mastheads.

My friend told me that this kind of ship is called a **freighter** because it carries cargo instead of passengers, like most other ships do these days. She said that sometimes you can see people **working** on deck even while the ship is moving through the harbor— can you imagine?—but today there wasn't anyone visible **onboard** except for up in the crow's nest where someone was on lookout duty high above everything else happening down below him on deck level. After watching the **harbour** activity for a while, we decided to walk around and explore. Hamburg is a big city, and there was so much to see. We walked down narrow streets lined with shops and cafes, past

beschlossen wir, ein wenig herumzulaufen und die Stadt zu erkunden. Hamburg ist eine große Stadt, und es gab so viel zu sehen. Wir spazierten durch schmale Straßen mit Geschäften und Cafés, vorbei an Kirchen und Regierungsgebäuden, bis wir schließlich am berühmten Fischmarkt ankamen. Der Markt war bereits in vollem Gange, obwohl es noch früh **am Morgen war**. Die Verkäufer riefen ihre Waren in einer Mischung aus **Deutsch** und Englisch an und versuchten, Kunden an ihre Stände zu locken. Die Luft war dick mit dem Geruch von Meeresfrüchten - einige
frisch und köstlich duftend, andere nicht so sehr.

Aber das alles trug zu der **festlichen** Atmosphäre des Ortes bei. Wir schlenderten eine Weile herum und nahmen alle Sehenswürdigkeiten und Geräusche (und Gerüche!) des Marktes in uns auf, bevor wir uns schließlich entschlossen, bei einem der Verkäufer, die **gegrillte** Garnelenspieße anboten, etwas **zu essen**. Nach dem Mittagessen gingen wir zurück zum Hafengebiet und beschlossen, eine Fahrt mit einem der Ausflugsboote zu machen, die Touren durch den Hafen anbieten. Das war eine tolle Möglichkeit, alles aus der Nähe zu sehen und mehr über die Geschichte **Hamburgs** und seines Hafens zu erfahren. Wir fuhren an allen möglichen Schiffen vorbei - Frachtern, Passagierschiffen und sogar einigen alten Segelschiffen, die aussahen, als gehörten sie in ein Museum.

churches and government buildings, until we finally arrived at the famous fish market. The market was already in full swing, even though it was still early **morning**. Vendors were shouting out their wares in a mix of **German** and English, trying to lure customers over to their stalls. The air was thick with the smell of seafood—some
fresh and delicious-smelling, others not so much.

But it all added to the **festive** atmosphere of the place. We wandered around for awhile, taking in all the sights and sounds (and smells!) of the market before finally deciding to buy some **lunch** from one of the vendors selling **grilled** shrimp skewers. After lunch, we walked back down to the harbour area and decided to go for a ride on one of the **sightseeing** boats that give tours of the harbor. It was a great way to see everything up close and learn more about the history of **Hamburg** and its harbor. We cruised past all sorts of different ships—freighters, passenger liners, even some old sailing ships that looked like they belonged in a museum.

Verständnisfragen

1. Wie heißt die Stadt, die der Autor besucht hat?

2. Was hielt der Autor von den Menschen in Köln?

3. Wie heißt die berühmte Kathedrale in Köln?

4. Was hält der Autor von der Kathedrale?

5. Was hat der Autor in der Kathedrale gemacht?

6. Wie fand der Autor die Aussicht vom Turm der Kathedrale?

7. Was hat der Autor zu Abend gegessen?

8. Wo befand sich das Restaurant?

9. Wie fand der Autor das Essen?

Comprehension Questions

1. What is the name of the city the author visited?

2. What did the author think of the people in Cologne?

3. What is the name of the famous cathedral in Cologne?

4. What did the author think of the cathedral?

5. What did the author do at the cathedral?

6. What did the author think of the view from the top of the cathedral tower?

7. What did the author have for dinner?

8. Where was the restaurant located?

9. What did the author think of the food?

Der Schwarzwald

Als ich den Schwarzwald betrete, werde ich sofort von der Dunkelheit eingehüllt. Die **Bäume** stehen so dicht **beieinander**, dass sie das meiste Licht ausblenden, und das einzige Geräusch ist das Knirschen der Blätter unter meinen Füßen. Ich spüre eine **Vorahnung**, als ich immer tiefer in den **Wald eindringe**, und bald kann ich den Weg hinter mir nicht mehr sehen. Ich gehe weiter, obwohl ich nicht sicher bin, wohin ich gehe oder was ich finden werde. Plötzlich bewegt sich etwas vor mir, und ich zucke erschrocken zurück. Es ist nur ein Reh, aber es erschreckt mich trotzdem. Während es davonhüpft, denke ich darüber nach, wie leicht man sich hier verlaufen kann. Ich wandere weiter durch den Schwarzwald und behalte
halten Sie Ausschau nach Anzeichen von **Zivilisation**.

Die Sonne geht langsam unter, und ich weiß, dass ich bald einen Unterschlupf finden muss. Ich höre ein Rascheln im **Gebüsch** und werde nervös, aber es ist nur ein weiteres Reh. Ich entspanne mich etwas, **gehe** aber weiter. Es wird jetzt dunkel, und ich habe immer noch keine Spur gefunden, die einer Fährte ähnelt. Plötzlich sehe ich in der Ferne ein Licht und **laufe darauf zu**. Als ich näher komme, sehe ich, dass es aus einer Hütte kommt. Erleichterung macht sich in mir breit, als ich zur Hütte gehe und an die Tür klopfe. Nach ein paar **Augenblicken öffnet** eine alte Frau die Tür. Sie sieht **überrascht** aus, mich zu sehen, aber sie bittet mich herein und bietet mir an, einen Tee zu

The Black Forest

As I step into the Black Forest, I am immediately enveloped in darkness. The **trees** are so close **together** that they block out most of the light, and the only sound is the crunching of leaves under my feet. I have a feeling of **foreboding** as I walk deeper into the **woods**, and soon I can no longer see the path behind me. I keep walking, though I am not sure where I am going or what I will find. Suddenly, something moves in front of me, and I jump back with a gasp. It is just a deer, but it startles me nonetheless. As it bounds away, I think about how easy it would be to get lost in this place. I continue to hike through the Black Forest, keeping
a close eye out for any sign of **civilization**.

The sun is starting to set, and I know I need to find shelter soon. I hear a rustling in the **bushes** and tense up, but it's just another deer. I relax slightly, but keep **moving**. It's getting dark now, and I still haven't found anything resembling a trail. Suddenly, I see a light in the distance and start **walking** towards it. As I get closer, I see that it is coming from a cabin. Relief washes over me as I walk up to the cabin and knock on the door. After a few **moments**, an old woman answers the door. She looks **surprised** to see me, but she invites me in and offers to make some tea. I gratefully accepted her offer and sat down by the fire. The old woman begins to tell me about the **forest**. She says that it is a magical place, full of secrets and wonders. She tells me about the time she saw a unicorn in the forest, and I can't help

kochen. Ich nehme ihr Angebot dankend an und setze mich ans Feuer. Die alte Frau beginnt, mir von dem **Wald zu erzählen**. Sie sagt, es sei ein magischer Ort, voller Geheimnisse und Wunder. Sie erzählt mir, dass sie einmal ein Einhorn im Wald gesehen hat, und ich kann nicht anders, als ihr zu glauben. Während wir so dasitzen und reden, fühle ich, wie meine Sorgen dahinschmelzen.

Ich war gerade dabei, mich zu entspannen, als ich plötzlich **draußen** ein Geräusch hörte. Es hört sich an, als würde etwas **auf die** Hütte zukommen. Ich schnappe mir schnell mein Messer und verstecke mich hinter der Tür. Als ich durch den Spalt spähe, sehe ich einen großen schwarzen Bären auf seinen Hinterbeinen laufen. Er schnüffelt herum und scheint mich noch nicht gesehen zu haben. Ich bin mir nicht sicher, was ich tun soll. Ich warte, was **mir** wie eine Ewigkeit vorkommt, aber schließlich geht der Bär weg. Ich stoße einen Seufzer der Erleichterung aus und lege mein Messer weg. Einfach
Als ich gerade wieder ins Bett gehen will, höre ich draußen **etwas** anderes. Diesmal hört es sich an, als würden Leute reden. Ich nehme wieder mein **Messer** und schleiche zum Fenster, um zu sehen, wer es ist. Es ist eine Gruppe von dunkel gekleideten Männern, die ihre Gesichter bedeckt haben. Sie **tragen** große Säcke, und es sieht so aus, als ob sie auf das Haus nebenan zugehen würden. Ich weiß nicht, was sie vorhaben, aber es kann nichts Gutes sein. Schnell schleiche ich mich vom Fenster weg und gehe die **Treppe** wieder hinunter.

but believe her. As we sit there talking, I feel my worries melting away.

I was finally starting to relax when suddenly, I heard a noise **outside**. It sounds like something is coming **towards** the cabin. I quickly grab my knife and hide behind the door. Peeking through the crack, I see a large black bear walking on its hind legs. It's sniffing around and doesn't seem to have seen me yet. I'm not sure what to do. I wait for what **seems** like forever, but the bear finally wanders off. I let out a sigh of relief and put my knife away. Just
As I'm about to go back to bed, I hear **something** else outside. This time it sounds like people are talking. I grab my **knife** again and creep towards the window to see who it is. It's a group of men in dark clothing, with their faces covered. They're **carrying** large sacks, and it looks like they're headed towards the house next door. I don't know what they're up to, but it can't be good. I quickly sneak away from the window and head back down the **stairs**.

Verständnisfragen

1. Wie heißt die Stadt, die der Autor besucht hat?

2. Was hielt der Autor von den Menschen in Köln?

3. Wie heißt die berühmte Kathedrale in Köln?

4. Was hält der Autor von der Kathedrale?

5. Was hat der Autor in der Kathedrale gemacht?

6. Was hält der Autor von der Aussicht von der Spitze der Kathedrale?

7. Was hat der Autor zu Abend gegessen?

8. Wo war das Restaurant?

9. Wie hat der Autor das Essen empfunden?

Comprehension Questions

1. What is the name of the city the author visited?

2. What did the author think of the people in Cologne?

3. What is the name of the famous cathedral in Cologne?

4. What did the author think of the cathedral?

5. What did the author do in the cathedral?

6. What did the author think about the view from the top of the cathedral?

7. What did the author have for dinner?

8. Where was the restaurant?

9. How did the author feel about the meal?

Kölner Dom

Ich wollte schon immer einmal Köln besuchen. Ich hatte schon so viel über die Stadt und ihren berühmten Dom gehört. Als ich eingeladen wurde, an einer Konferenz teilzunehmen, bekam ich endlich die Gelegenheit dazu. Ich kam an einem sonnigen Tag im Juni in Köln an. Das erste, was mir auffiel, war, wie sauber und gut gepflegt die Stadt war. **Überall, wo** ich hinsah, gab es Blumen und Bäume. Und die Menschen! Sie waren so freundlich und hilfsbereit, immer bereit, stehen zu bleiben und zu plaudern oder mir den Weg zu zeigen. Ich hatte gehört, dass die **Kathedrale** wirklich eine beeindruckende Sehenswürdigkeit ist. Seine gewaltige Größe ist **atemberaubend**, und im Inneren ist es so friedlich, trotz der Tausenden von Menschen, die ihn jeden Tag besuchen. Ich beschloss, den Kölner Dom zu besuchen, während ich in Köln war. Ich nahm den Bus von meinem Hotel und erreichte das **prächtige** Bauwerk innerhalb einer Stunde.

Nachdem ich eine Weile die Fassade bewundert hatte, ging ich hinein und war **von** der Größe des Gebäudes **überwältigt**. Es war ein unwirkliches Gefühl, an einem so historischen Ort zu stehen. Ich spazierte durch die Kathedrale, bewunderte ihre schöne Architektur und erfuhr etwas über ihre Geschichte. Ich besuchte auch die Schatzkammer, in der viele unschätzbare Artefakte aufbewahrt werden. Ich war **sofort** von der hoch aufragenden gotischen **Architektur** beeindruckt. Nachdem ich einige Minuten lang die Außenfassade bewundert hatte, machte ich mich auf den Weg

Cologne Cathedral

I had always wanted to visit Cologne. I had heard so much about the city and its famous cathedral. I finally got my chance when I was invited to attend a conference there. I arrived in Cologne on a sunny day in June. The first thing that **struck** me was how clean and well- maintained the city was. **Everywhere** I looked, there were flowers and trees. And the people! They were so friendly and helpful, always willing to stop and chat or offer directions. I had heard the **cathedral** is truly an amazing sight. Its massive size is **breathtaking**, and it's so peaceful inside, despite the thousands of people who visit it every day. I decided to visit Cologne Cathedral while I was in Cologne. I took the bus from my hotel and arrived at the **magnificent** structure within an hour.

After admiring its façade for a while, I went inside and was **awestruck** by its size. It felt surreal to be standing in such a historic place. I walked around the cathedral, admiring its beautiful architecture and learning about its history. I also visited the treasury, which houses many priceless artifacts. I was **immediately** impressed by the soaring Gothic **architecture**. After admiring the exterior for a few minutes, I made my way inside. The interior of the cathedral was even more breathtaking than the outside. The cavernous space was illuminated by **sunlight** streaming in through stained glass windows. I spent some time **walking** around and taking in all the details of this incredible building before making my way to the top of one of its towers. From up high,

ins Innere. Das Innere der Kathedrale war sogar noch atemberaubender als die Außenansicht. Der höhlenartige Raum wurde durch **Sonnenlicht** erhellt, das durch die Buntglasfenster hereinfiel. Ich verbrachte einige Zeit damit, herumzulaufen und alle Details dieses unglaublichen Gebäudes in mich aufzunehmen, bevor ich mich auf die Spitze eines der Türme begab. Von dort oben hatte ich einen atemberaubenden Blick auf Köln und die Umgebung. Nachdem ich die Aussicht eine Weile genossen hatte, stieg ich wieder auf den Boden hinunter und erkundete den Rest dieses erstaunlichen Ortes, eines der bekanntesten und schönsten **Gebäude** in Deutschland, das ich endlich aus der Nähe sehen konnte.

Ich wurde nicht **enttäuscht**. Ich verbrachte Stunden damit, im Inneren herumzulaufen und die Handwerkskunst zu **bewundern**. Ich kletterte auch auf die Spitze eines der Türme, um einen unglaublichen Blick auf die
Stadt unter uns. Als ich die Kathedrale verließ, war ich von dem, was ich gesehen hatte, einfach **überwältigt**. Es war ein unvergessliches Erlebnis, und ich bin so froh, dass ich diesen erstaunlichen Ort sehen konnte! Um 19 Uhr war ich hungrig und beschloss, dass es Zeit war, zu Abend zu essen. Als ich in mein Hotelzimmer zurückkam, war ich am Verhungern. Ich ging **hinunter** in die Lobby und fragte den **Concierge**, ob es in der Nähe ein gutes Restaurant gäbe, in dem ich etwas essen könnte.

I had a stunning view of Cologne and beyond. After enjoying the views for awhile, I descended back down to ground level and continued exploring the rest of this amazing place.It is one of the most iconic and beautiful **buildings** in Germany, and I finally had a chance to see it up close.

I was not **disappointed**. I spent hours walking around inside, **admiring** the craftsmanship. I also climbed to the top of one of the towers for an incredible view of the city below. As I left the cathedral, I couldn't help but feel **overwhelmed** by what I had seen. It was an unforgettable experience, and I'm so glad I got to see this amazing place!
By 7 pm, I was hungry and decided it was time to get dinner. I was starving by the time I got back to my hotel room. I went **downstairs** to the lobby and asked the **concierge** if there were any good places nearby to get some food.

Verständnisfragen

1. Wie heißt die Stadt, die der Autor besucht hat?

2. Was hielt der Autor von den Menschen in Köln?

3. Wie heißt die berühmte Kathedrale in Köln?

4. Was hält der Autor von der Kathedrale?

5. Was hat der Autor in der Kathedrale gemacht?

6. Wie fand der Autor die Aussicht vom Turm der Kathedrale?

Comprehension Questions

1. What is the name of the city the author visited?

2. What did the author think of the people in Cologne?

3. What is the name of the famous cathedral in Cologne?

4. What did the author think of the cathedral?

5. What did the author do at the cathedral?

6. What did the author think of the view from the top of the cathedral tower?

Besuch in Berlin

Ich wollte schon immer mal nach Berlin. Ich hatte schon so viel über die Stadt gehört - die Geschichte, die Kultur, das Essen. Als sich mir dann endlich die Gelegenheit bot, die Stadt zu besuchen, ergriff ich die Gelegenheit. Ich kam an einem kalten, grauen **Januartag** in Berlin an. Aber selbst das Wetter konnte meine Laune nicht trüben. Ich war begeistert, hier zu sein. Ich begann meine Erkundung der Stadt mit der **Besichtigung** einiger ihrer berühmtesten **Wahrzeichen**. Das Brandenburger Tor, der Reichstag, Checkpoint Charlie - all diese Orte hatte ich bisher nur auf Fotos oder im Fernsehen gesehen. Und jetzt war ich tatsächlich hier und stand vor ihnen. Ich verbrachte ein paar Tage damit, durch die Straßen Berlins zu schlendern und die **Sehenswürdigkeiten** und Geräusche dieser erstaunlichen Stadt in mich aufzunehmen. Ich aß Currywurst und trank Bier in Biergärten.

Ich habe Museen und **Kunstgalerien** besucht. Ich habe sogar eine Bootsfahrt auf der Spree gemacht. Ich habe mir auch einige weniger bekannte Orte angesehen, wie den **Mauerpark** und die East Side **Gallery**. Ich war wirklich beeindruckt, wie viel Geschichte es in Berlin gibt. Jede Ecke schien eine Geschichte zu erzählen zu haben. Ich fand es toll, etwas über die Vergangenheit der Stadt und all die **verschiedenen** Kulturen zu erfahren, die sie beeinflusst haben. Ich habe auch das Essen und das Nachtleben in Berlin genossen. Es gibt so viele tolle Restaurants und Bars, aus denen man

Visiting Berlin

I'd always wanted to visit Berlin. I'd heard so much about the city—the history, the culture, the food. And so, when I finally had the opportunity to visit, I jumped at the chance. I arrived in Berlin on a cold, grey day in **January**. But even the weather couldn't dampen my spirits. I was excited to be here. I started my exploration of the city by **visiting** some of its most famous **landmarks**. The Brandenburg Gate, the Reichstag, Checkpoint Charlie – these were all places I'd only ever seen in photos or on TV. And now I was actually here, standing in front of them. I spent a few days just wandering the streets of Berlin, taking in the **sights** and sounds of this amazing city. I ate currywurst and drank beer in beer gardens.

I visited museums and art **galleries**. I even took a boat ride down the River Spree. I also made sure to check out some of the lesser-known spots, like the **Mauerpark** and the East Side **Gallery**. I was really impressed by how much history there is in Berlin. Every corner seemed to have a story to tell. I loved learning about the city's past and all the **different** cultures that have influenced it. I also enjoyed the food and nightlife in Berlin. There are so many great restaurants and bars to choose from.I walked into the bar and immediately felt a bit out of place. It was too bright, too loud, and everyone seemed to be **having** way too much fun. I ordered a **beer** and sat down at a table by myself. I people-watched for a while, wondering what their stories were.

wählen kann. Ich betrat die Bar und fühlte mich sofort fehl am Platz. Es war zu hell, zu laut, und alle schienen viel zu viel Spaß zu haben. Ich bestellte ein **Bier** und setzte mich allein an einen Tisch. Ich beobachtete die Leute eine Weile und fragte mich, was ihre Geschichten waren. Waren sie Einheimische oder Touristen? Was machten sie in Berlin? Während ich an meinem Bier nippte, begann ich mich zu entspannen und die Atmosphäre zu genießen. Das war der Grund, warum ich Berlin liebte - es war immer so lebendig und es gab immer **etwas** Neues zu entdecken. Die **Musik** begann in meinem Körper zu pulsieren, und ich konnte nicht anders, als mit dem Fuß mitzuwippen. Es dauerte nicht lange, und ich erhob mich von meinem Platz und tanzte allein in der Mitte des Lokals. Niemand kümmerte sich darum, dass ich niemanden kannte - sie waren alle zu sehr damit beschäftigt, sich zu amüsieren. Ich verließ die Bar lächelnd und war glücklich, eine andere Seite Berlins kennengelernt zu haben, von der ich gar nicht wusste, dass sie existiert.

Ich wollte etwas von der lokalen Küche probieren. Ich stellte einige Nachforschungen an und fand ein Restaurant, das **vielversprechend** schien. Ich beschloss, eines Abends dorthin zum **Abendessen zu** gehen. Das **Restaurant befand** sich in einem belebten Viertel der Stadt. Als ich ankam, war es sehr voll, aber ich konnte einen Tisch bekommen. Die Speisekarte bot eine große Auswahl, und ich brauchte eine Weile, um mich zu entscheiden, was ich bestellen wollte. Schließlich **entschied ich mich** für ein **traditionelles** deutsches Gericht: Sauerkraut, Wurst und Kartoffeln.

Were they locals or tourists? What were they doing in Berlin? As I sipped my beer, I started to relax and enjoy the atmosphere. This was why I loved Berlin—it was always so alive and there was always **something** new to discover. The **music** started to pulse through my body, and I couldn't help but tap my foot along with it. Before long, I was up out of my seat, dancing by myself in the middle of the bar. Nobody cared that I didn't know anyone – they were all too busy enjoying themselves. I left the bar smiling, feeling happy to have experienced another side of Berlin that I never knew existed.

I wanted to try some of the local cuisine. I did some research and found a restaurant that seemed **promising**. I decided to go there for **dinner** one evening. The **restaurant** was located in a busy area of the city. It was crowded when I arrived, but I was able to get a table. The menu had a lot of options, and it took me a while to decide what to order. I finally **settled** on some **traditional** German food: sauerkraut, sausage, and potatoes.

Verständnisfragen

1. Wie war das Wetter, als der Autor in Berlin ankam?

2. Welche Orte hat der Autor während seines Aufenthalts in Berlin besucht?

3. Wie fand der Autor das Essen in Berlin?

4. Welchen Eindruck hatte der Autor von den Menschen in Berlin?

5. Wie fand der Autor das Nachtleben in Berlin?

6. Was hält der Autor von der Geschichte der Stadt?

7. Was hat dem Autor an seinem Besuch in Berlin am besten gefallen?

8. Was hat der Autor zum Abendessen im Restaurant bestellt?

Comprehension Questions

1. What was the weather like when the author arrived in Berlin?

2. What are some of the places the author visited while in Berlin?

3. What did the author think of the food in Berlin?

4. What was the author's impression of the people in Berlin?

5. What did the author think of the nightlife in Berlin?

6. What did the author think of the city's history?

7. What was the author's favorite part of visiting Berlin?

8. What did the author order for dinner at the restaurant?.

Fußballspiel

Als junger Amerikaner habe ich mich nie wirklich für Fußball interessiert. Ich wusste zwar davon, und ich hatte ein paar Spiele im Fernsehen gesehen, aber es **hat** mich nie wirklich interessiert. Als ich jedoch nach Deutschland zog, um zu studieren, begann ich eine echte Liebe für diesen Sport zu entwickeln. Und wo könnte man besser **Fußball** sehen als in Deutschland, wo einige der besten Mannschaften der Welt zu Hause sind? Als mir ein Freund von einem Fußballspiel in Berlin erzählte, wusste ich, dass ich unbedingt hingehen musste. Ich war noch nie zuvor bei einem Spiel gewesen, geschweige denn bei einem Fußballspiel, aber ich war **gespannt darauf**, etwas Neues zu erleben. Das **Spiel** war unglaublich. Tausende von Menschen aus ganz Deutschland (und sogar einige aus anderen Ländern) kamen zusammen, um ihre Liebe zum Fußball zu feiern. Es waren so viele verschiedene Mannschaften vertreten, und alle sangen und skandierten gemeinsam. Es war eine unglaubliche Atmosphäre.

Damals wusste ich noch nicht viel über den deutschen Fußball, aber ich erfuhr schnell, dass Bayern München die beliebteste Mannschaft war. Und wie sich herausstellte, spielten sie auch im **Endspiel**. Es war in den frühen Morgenstunden, als wir in Frankfurt ankamen. Die Stadt schlief noch, aber wir konnten die Aufregung in der Luft spüren. Wir machten uns auf den Weg zum Treffpunkt, wo sich bereits Menschen

Football Match

As a young American, I was never really into football. I knew of it, and I had seen a few games on television, but it never really **caught** my interest. However, when I moved to Germany for college, I started to develop a real love for the sport. And what better place to watch **football** than in Germany, the home of some of the best teams in the world? So, when a friend told me about a **football** match that was happening in Berlin, I knew that I had to go. I had never been to a match before, let alone a football match, but I was **excited** to experience something new. The **match** was incredible. Thousands of people from all over Germany (and even some from other countries) came together to celebrate their love for football. There were so many different teams represented, and everyone was chanting and singing together. It was an amazing atmosphere.

I didn't know much about German football at the time, but I quickly learned that Bayern Munich were the most popular team. And, as it turns out, they were also playing in the **final** game. It was the early **hours** of the morning when we arrived in Frankfurt. The city was still asleep, but we could feel the excitement in the air. We made our way to the meeting point, where people were already **starting** to gather. We joined the crowd and began to march. The sun was rising as we made our way through the streets of **Frankfurt**. The closer we got to the **stadium**, the more people joined us. By the time we arrived, the stadium was overflowing with people. We chanted and sang as we marched around the

versammelten. Wir schlossen uns der Menge an und begannen zu marschieren. Die Sonne ging gerade auf, als wir durch die Straßen von **Frankfurt zogen**. Je näher wir dem **Stadion kamen**, desto mehr Menschen schlossen sich uns an. Als wir dort ankamen, war das Stadion überfüllt mit Menschen. Wir sangen und skandierten, während wir um das Stadion marschierten. Die **Atmosphäre** war elektrisierend. Wir konnten die Kraft der Menschen um uns herum spüren. Wir waren vereint in unserer Liebe für unser Team und unser Land. Der Marsch ging noch stundenlang weiter, aber schließlich war es Zeit, nach Hause zu gehen. Wir verließen das Stadion, unsere Stimmen klangen noch in unseren Ohren.

Wir haben heute Geschichte geschrieben. Wir haben der Welt gezeigt, dass Deutschland eine Kraft ist, mit der man **rechnen muss**. Ich war in **Deutschland**, als die Weltmeisterschaft dort stattfand. Es war ein wunderschöner Tag für einen Fußballmarsch. Die Sonne schien und die **deutschen** Fans waren in voller Montur unterwegs. Sie waren alle in den Farben ihrer Mannschaften gekleidet und sangen und skandierten, während sie gingen. Es war ein Meer aus Rot, Weiß und Schwarz. Der Marsch zog sich über Stunden hin, aber es war die Mühe wert, als die Mannschaft endlich herauskam. Die **Spieler** lächelten und winkten der **Menge zu**. Sie sahen aus, als wären sie bereit, es mit der Welt aufzunehmen. Das Spiel war spannend. Wir machten uns früh am Morgen auf den Weg durch die Stadt. Die Straßen waren voll mit Menschen, die alle die Farben ihrer Mannschaft trugen.

stadium. The **atmosphere** was electric. We could feel the power of the people around us. We were united in our love for our team and our country. The march went on for hours, but eventually, it was time to go home. We left the stadium, our voices still ringing in our ears.

We have made history today. We have shown the world that Germany is a force to be **reckoned** with. Iwas in **Germany** when the World Cup was held there. It was a beautiful day for a football march. The sun was shining and the **German** fans were out in full force. They were all decked out in their team colors, chanting and singing as they went. It was a sea of red, white, and black. The march went on for hours, but it was all worth it when the team finally came out. The **players** were all smiles as they waved to the **crowd**. They looked like they were ready to take on the world. The game was electric. We started early in the morning, making our way through the city. The streets were packed with people, all wearing their team's colors.

Verständnisfragen

1. Wie war die Atmosphäre im Stadion?

2. Wie hat sich der Autor gefühlt, als er das Spiel miterleben konnte?

3. Was war das einprägsamste Erlebnis für den Autor?

4. Wie war es für den Autor, die Mannschaft herauskommen zu sehen?

5. Wie war das noch gleich?

6. Wie war es für den Autor, an dem Marsch teilzunehmen?

7. Wie hat der Autor die Erfahrung insgesamt empfunden?

8. Wie war die Stimmung in der Menge?

Comprehension Questions

1. What was the atmosphere like in the stadium?

2. How did the author feel about being able to witness the match?

3. What was the most memorable experience for the author?

4. What was it like for the author to see the team come out?

5. What was the like?

6. What was it like for the author to be a part of the march?

7. What did the author think of the experience overall?

8. What was the crowd like?

Oktoberfest

Jedes Jahr strömen **Hunderttausende** von Menschen zum Oktoberfest, dem **größten Volksfest** der Welt, nach München. Die Veranstaltung ist ein Fest der bayerischen Kultur, das zwei **Wochen lang dauert** und am ersten Oktoberwochenende seinen Höhepunkt erreicht. Für viele Menschen ist das Oktoberfest eine Gelegenheit, sich auszutoben und kräftig zu feiern. Die Bierzelte sind immer voll, und es ist nicht **ungewöhnlich, dass man** Leute sieht, die herumstolpern und kaum stehen können. Aber das Oktoberfest ist auch eine familienfreundliche Veranstaltung mit vielen Aktivitäten für Kinder. Ich wollte schon immer mal auf das Oktoberfest gehen, aber ich habe es nicht geschafft, bis

Ich war Anfang **zwanzig**, als ich endlich die Reise antrat. Ich reiste mit einer Gruppe von Freunden, und wir hatten eine tolle Zeit. Wir begannen unsere Tage damit, **München** zu erkunden und einige **Sehenswürdigkeiten zu besichtigen**. Am Nachmittag fuhren wir dann zum Oktoberfestgelände und blieben dort bis spät in die Nacht.

Wir probierten all die **verschiedenen** Bierzelte aus und aßen viele traditionelle bayerische Gerichte. Wir gingen auch auf einige der Fahrgeschäfte, die überraschenderweise nicht so überfüllt waren, wie ich dachte. Der Geruch von frischen **Brezeln** und Bier erfüllte die Luft, als ich mir meinen Weg durch die Oktoberfest-Massen bahnte. Ich konnte mir ein Lächeln

Oktoberfest

Every year, hundreds of **thousands** of people descend upon Munich for Oktoberfest, the world's **largest** fair. The event is a celebration of Bavarian culture and lasts for two **weeks**, culminating in the first weekend of October. For many people, Octoberfest is a chance to let loose and party hard. The beer tents are always packed, and it's not **uncommon** to see people stumbling around, barely able to stand. But Octoberfest is also a family- friendly event, with plenty of activities for children. I had always wanted to go to Oktoberfest, but it wasn't until
I was in my early **twenties** that I finally made the trip. I went with a group of friends, and we had an amazing time. We started our days by exploring **Munich** and doing some **sightseeing**. We would then head to the Octoberfest grounds in the afternoon and stay there until late at night.

We tried out all the **different** beer tents and ate lots of traditional Bavarian food. We also went on some of the rides, which were surprisingly not as crowded as I thought they would be. The smell of fresh **pretzels** and beer filled the air as I made my way through the Oktoberfest crowds. I couldn't help but smile as I took in the festive **atmosphere** — people were laughing and dancing everywhere I looked. I bought a stein of beer and found a spot to people- watch. I watched as groups of friends toasted each other, clinking their glasses together and taking big gulps of beer. The sounds of

nicht verkneifen, als ich die festliche **Atmosphäre in mich** aufnahm - überall lachten und tanzten die Leute. Ich kaufte mir einen Krug Bier und suchte mir einen Platz, um die Leute zu beobachten. Ich beobachtete, wie Gruppen von Freunden aufeinander anstießen, ihre Gläser aneinander stießen und große Schlucke Bier nahmen. Lachen und Musik erfüllten die Luft, und ich konnte nicht anders, als mit dem Fuß im Takt zu wippen. Plötzlich rempelte mich jemand von hinten an und **verschüttete** mein Bier über mein Hemd. Ich drehte mich um und sah eine Gruppe rüpelhafter Jugendlicher, die offensichtlich schon ziemlich betrunken waren. Sie **entschuldigten sich** vielmals und boten mir an, mir ein neues Bier zu kaufen. Ich lehnte ab, aber sie bestanden darauf, und so gab ich schließlich nach.

 Ich unterhielt mich eine Weile mit ihnen und fand heraus, dass sie alle aus verschiedenen Teilen Deutschlands stammen. Sie **luden** mich an ihren Tisch **ein**, und ich hatte viel Spaß beim **Tanzen** und Trinken mit ihnen bis in die Nacht hinein. Als die Sonne aufging, wurde mir klar, dass ich eine unglaubliche Zeit erlebt hatte - das war definitiv eine Nacht, die ich nie vergessen werde! Am liebsten habe ich auf dem Oktoberfest einfach nur Leute beobachtet. Es hat **etwas**, in einer so festlichen **Atmosphäre zu** sein, das einen einfach glücklich macht. Wenn Sie noch nie auf dem Oktoberfest waren, kann ich es nur empfehlen. Es ist eine einmalige Erfahrung, die man nicht bereuen wird.

laughter and music filled the air, and I couldn't help but tap my foot along to the beat. Suddenly, someone bumped into me from behind, **spilling** my beer all over my shirt. I turned around to see a group of rowdy teenagers, who were clearly already quite drunk. They **apologised** profusely and offered to buy me a new beer. I declined, but they insisted, so I eventually gave in.

 I chatted with them for a while and found out that they're all from different parts of Germany. They **invited** me to join their table, and I had a great time **dancing** and drinking with them into the night. As the sun started to come up, I realized that I'd had an incredible time – this was definitely a night that I'd never forget! My favorite part of Octoberfest was simply people watching. There's **something** about being in such a festive **atmosphere** that just makes you happy. If you've never been to Octoberfest, I would highly recommend it. It's a once in a lifetime experience that you won't regret.

Verständnisfragen

1. Wo findet jedes Jahr das Oktoberfest statt?

2. Wie viele Menschen besuchen jedes Jahr das Oktoberfest?

3. Wofür ist das Oktoberfest bekannt?

4. Wie lange dauert das Oktoberfest?

5. In welchem Monat findet das Oktoberfest statt?

6. Warum wollte der Autor das Oktoberfest besuchen?

7. Wie ist der Autor zum Oktoberfest gereist?

8. Was hat der Autor in den Bierzelten gemacht?

9. Welche Aktivitäten gab es für Kinder?

Comprehension Questions

1. Where is the Oktoberfest held every year?

2. How many people visit the Oktoberfest every year?

3. What is the Oktoberfest known for?

4. How long does the Oktoberfest last?

5. In which month is the Oktoberfest?

6. Why did the author want to visit the Oktoberfest?

7. How did the author travel to the Oktoberfest?

8. What did the author do in the beer tents?

9. What activities were there for children?

Am Strand

Nach Sonnenaufgang sind die Wellen lauter und der Sand oberhalb der Flut ist weiß. Ich gehe hinunter zum Strand, **bewundere** das Meer und die Sonne. Meine Zehen spüren die Rillen der Muscheln. Der Sand ist kalt an meinen Zehen. Ich lächle und gehe weiter. Die Flut ist hoch, also muss ich aufpassen, dass ich nicht hineingezogen werde. Ich laufe am Ufer entlang und bewundere das Meer. Der Sonnenaufgang ist **wunderschön**, und die Wellen plätschern. Ich fühle mich so friedlich. Ich komme zu einer Stelle, an der ein Felsvorsprung steht. Ich setze mich hin und beobachte die Wellen. Das Wasser ist so blau und der Himmel ist so **orange**. Ich fühle mich wie in einem Traum. Ich schließe die Augen und lausche einfach nur den Wellen. Ich saß lange Zeit dort, bis ich hörte, wie jemand meinen Namen rief.

Ich öffne meine Augen und sehe meine Mutter auf mich zukommen. Sie hat einen besorgten Ausdruck im Gesicht. Ich lächle und winke, und sie **entspannt sich**. "Ich habe mich schon gefragt, wo du bist", sagt sie. "Ich freue mich, dass du den Strand genießt." Ich antworte: "Das tue ich." "Es ist so schön hier." "Ich weiß", sagt sie. "Als ich in deinem Alter war, bin ich ständig hierhergekommen." "Wirklich?" frage ich. "Ja", antwortet sie. "Es ist ein besonderer Ort.""Hast du hier jemals jemand Besonderen getroffen?" frage ich. "Ja", antwortet sie mit einem Lächeln. "Deinen Vater." "Wirklich?" sage ich **erstaunt**. "Ja", sagt sie. "Wir waren

At the beach

After sunrise, the waves are louder and the sand above
the tide is white. I walk down to the beach, **admiring**
the sea and the sun. My toes feel the grooves of shells.
The sand is cold on my toes. I smile and keep going.
The tide is high, so I have to be careful not to get pulled
in. I walk along the water's edge, admiring the sea.
The sunrise is **beautiful**, and the waves are crashing. I
feel so peaceful. I come to a spot where there is a rock
outcropping. I sit down and watch the waves. The water
is so blue and the sky is so **orange**. I feel like I'm in a
dream. I close my eyes and just listen to the waves. I
sat there for a long time, until I heard someone calling
my name.

I open my eyes and see my mom walking towards me.
She has a worried look on her face. I smile and wave,
and she **relaxes**. "I was wondering where you went,"
she says. "I'm glad you're enjoying the beach." I reply,
"I am." "It's so beautiful here." "I know," she says. "I
used to come here all the time when I was your age."
"Really?" I ask. "Yeah," she replies. "It's a special
place.""Did you ever meet anyone special here?" I ask.
"I did," she replies with a smile. "Your father." "Really?"
I say, **surprised**. "Yes," she says. "We used to come
here all the time together. It's where we fell in love. "
I smile, **imagining** my parents falling in love on this
beautiful beach. "It's a special place," she repeats. "I'm
glad you came here today."

We sit there for a while longer, **watching** the waves and

früher immer zusammen hier. Hier haben wir uns verliebt. "Ich lächle und **stelle mir** meine Eltern **vor, wie sie sich** an diesem schönen Strand verlieben. "Es ist ein besonderer Ort", wiederholt sie. "Ich bin froh, dass du heute hierher gekommen bist."

Wir sitzen noch eine Weile da und **beobachten** die Wellen und den Sonnenuntergang. Dann stehen wir auf und gehen zurück zu unseren Strandtüchern. Ich lege mich hin und schaue mir die Sterne an. Ich fühle mich so glücklich und zufrieden. Die Wellen sind jetzt lauter, und der Sand ist kalt. Die Sonne geht unter und eine kühle Brise weht. Die Wellen schlagen gegen das Ufer, und der Geruch von Salz liegt in der Luft. Es ist ein perfekter Abend, um am Strand zu sein. Ich spaziere am Ufer entlang, **lausche dem** Rauschen der Wellen und beobachte den Sonnenuntergang. Ich sehe eine Gruppe von Leuten, die lachend und scherzend im Sand sitzen. Sie sehen aus, als hätten sie eine tolle Zeit. Ich gehe zu ihnen hin und frage, ob ich mich zu ihnen setzen darf. Sie sagen ja, und wir verbringen den Rest des Abends damit, uns zu unterhalten, zu lachen und den **Sonnenuntergang** zu beobachten. Es ist ein perfekter Abend. Die Gruppe und ich unterhalten uns, bis die Sonne untergeht. Wir tauschen Geschichten und Witze aus und haben alle eine tolle Zeit. Als die Nacht hereinbricht, werden wir alle langsam müde. Wir küssen uns **zum Abschied** und trennen uns. Ich gehe glücklich und zufrieden zurück in mein Hotel. Ich kann nicht glauben, wie schön es hier ist. Ich bin so glücklich, dass ich das **erleben durfte.**

the sunset. Then we get up and walk back to our beach towels. I lie down and look at the stars. I feel so happy and content. The waves are louder now, and the sand is cold. The sun is setting and a cool breeze is blowing. The waves are crashing against the shore, and the smell of salt is in the air. It is a perfect evening to be at the beach.

I am walking along the shore, **listening** to the sound of the waves and watching the sunset. I see a group of people sitting on the sand, laughing and joking around. They look like they are having a great time. I walk over to them and ask if I can join them. They say yes, and we spend the rest of the evening talking, laughing, and watching the **sunset**. It is a perfect evening. The group and I talk until the sun sets. We share stories and jokes, and we all have a great time. As the night starts to fall, we all start to feel tired. We kiss each other **goodbye** and part ways. I walk back to my hotel, feeling happy and content. I can't believe how lovely it is here. I'm so lucky to have **experienced** it.

Verständnisfragen

1. Wohin geht die Erzählerin, nachdem sie aufgewacht ist?

2. Was bewundert die Erzählerin, während sie am Strand entlanggeht?

3. Worauf muss die Erzählerin aufpassen, wenn sie am Strand entlanggeht?

4. Wo setzt sich der Erzähler hin, um die Aussicht zu genießen?

5. Wie lange sitzt der Erzähler dort?

6. Wen sieht die Erzählerin, als sie ihre Augen wieder öffnet?

7. Was sagt die Mutter des Erzählers?

8. Worüber sprechen die Erzählerin und die Menschen, die sie trifft?

Comprehension Questions

1. Where does the narrator go after she wakes up?

2. What is the narrator admiring as she walks along the beach?

3. What does the narrator have to watch out for as she walks along the beach?

4. Where does the narrator sit down to enjoy the view?

5. How long does the narrator sit there?

6. Whom does the narrator see when she opens her eyes again?

7. What does the narrator's mother say?

8. What do the narrator and the people she meets talk about?

Camping am See

Ich gehe auf den See zu und **bewundere** die Ruhe, die hier herrscht. Die Sonne brennt auf den kleinen See und lässt das Wasser wie eine Glasscheibe aussehen. Die einzige Bewegung ist das gelegentliche Plätschern eines Fisches, der die Oberfläche durchbricht. Selbst die Vögel scheinen sich von der Hitze zu erholen, denn nur das Zirpen der Zikaden erfüllt die Luft. **Plötzlich wird** die Ruhe durch ein lautes Plätschern unterbrochen. Ein großer **Fisch ist aus dem** Wasser gesprungen und versucht, eine Libelle zu fangen. Der Fisch verfehlt sein Ziel und fällt mit einem Platschen zurück ins Wasser. "Wow", denke ich mir, "das war ein großer Fisch!". Ich schaue mich um, um zu sehen, ob ihn noch jemand gesehen hat, aber es ist niemand da. Ich werde es ihnen wohl erzählen müssen, wenn ich zum Camp zurückkehre.

Die Hitze ist **drückend** und macht das Atmen schwer. Die Luft ist dick und schwer, wie eine Decke, die einen einhüllt. Die einzige Erleichterung bietet das Wasser. Es ist kühl und erfrischend, wie ein kaltes Getränk an einem heißen Tag. Ich atme tief ein und tauche ins Wasser ein. Die Erleichterung tritt sofort ein, als mich das kühle Wasser umgibt. Ich schwimme auf den Grund und dann wieder an die Oberfläche und spüre, wie das Wasser meinen Körper kühlt. Ich **schwimme** weiter meine Runden und genieße die Abkühlung von der Hitze. Nach einer Weile steige ich aus dem Wasser und lege mich ins Gras, damit die Sonne meinen Körper

Camping at the Lake

I walk towards the lake, **admiring** the peacefulness of the scene. The sun is beating down on the small lake, making the water look like a sheet of glass. The only movement is the occasional ripple from a fish **breaking** the surface. Even the birds seem to be taking a break from the heat, with only the sound of cicadas filling the air. **Suddenly**, the peace is broken by a loud splash. A large **fish** has jumped out of the water, trying to catch a dragonfly. The fish misses its target and falls back into the water with a splash. "Wow," I think to myself, "that was a big fish!." I looked around to see if anyone else saw it, but there was no one around. I guess I'll have to tell them when I get back to camp.

The heat is **oppressive**, making it hard to breathe. The air is thick and heavy, like a blanket wrapped around you. The only relief is in the water. It is cool and refreshing, like a cold drink on a hot day. I take a deep breath and dive into the water. The relief is immediate as the cool water surrounds me. I swim down to the bottom and then back up to the surface, feeling the water cool my body. I continue **swimming** laps, enjoying the respite from the heat. After a while, I get out of the water and lie down on the grass, letting the sun dry my body. I close my eyes and drift off to sleep, the sound of the **cicadas** lulling me into a deep slumber. I let the sun bake the water out of my skin. I can feel my skin getting red, but I don't care. I am too hot to care.The next thing I know, the sun is setting.

trocknen kann. Ich schließe die Augen und schlafe ein. Das **Zirpen der Zikaden** wiegt mich in einen tiefen Schlaf. Ich lasse die Sonne das Wasser aus meiner Haut brennen. Ich spüre, wie meine Haut rot wird, aber es ist mir egal. Mir ist zu heiß, als dass es mir etwas ausmachen würde, und schon geht die Sonne unter. Der Himmel färbt sich orange mit rosa und violetten Reflexen. Die Hitze ist verschwunden und wird durch eine kühle **Brise** ersetzt.

Ich stehe auf und ziehe mich wieder an, fühle mich erfrischt und verjüngt. Ich **atme** tief die kühle Luft ein und lächle. Es ist ein gutes Gefühl, am Leben zu sein. Ich laufe zurück zum Campingplatz und bewundere, wie die Farben am Himmel tanzen. In der Ferne sehe ich das Lagerfeuer brennen und kann den Rauch in der Luft riechen. Ich lächle und **beschleunige** mein Tempo. Ich bin bereit, mich zu entspannen und den Rest des Abends zu genießen. Ich betrete den Lagerplatz und sehe, dass alle um das Feuer versammelt sind. Sie **lachen** und scherzen, und ich kann sehen, wie sich das Feuer in ihren Augen spiegelt. Ich lächle und setze mich neben meine Freunde. Es ist schön, wieder hier zu sein. Am nächsten Morgen wache ich früh auf und beginne, meine Sachen zu packen. Ich kann es kaum erwarten, mich wieder auf den Weg zu machen und meine Reise fortzusetzen. Ich verabschiede mich von meinen Freunden und mache mich auf den Weg. Während ich gehe, werfe ich einen letzten Blick auf den **Campingplatz**. Ich sehe das Feuer in der Ferne noch brennen und rieche den Rauch in der Luft. Ich lächle und beschleunige mein Tempo. Ich bin bereit, meine **Reise** fortzusetzen.

The sky is a beautiful orange, with streaks of pink and purple. The heat is gone, replaced by a cool **breeze**.

I get up and put my clothes back on, feeling refreshed and rejuvenated. I take a deep **breath** of the cool air and smile. It feels good to be alive. I walk back to the campsite, admiring the way the colors dance in the sky. I can see the campfire burning in the distance, and I can smell the smoke in the air. I smile and **quicken** my pace. I am ready to relax and enjoy the rest of my evening. I walk into the campsite and see that everyone is gathered around the fire. They are **laughing** and joking, and I can see the fire reflecting in their eyes. I smile and sit down next to my friends. It is good to be back. The next morning, I wake up early and start to pack up my things. I am eager to get back on the trail and continue my journey. I say goodbye to my friends and start to walk away. As I walk, I take one last look at the **campsite**. I can see the fire still burning in the distance, and I can smell the smoke in the air. I smile and quicken my pace. I'm ready to continue my **journey**.

Verständnisfragen

1. Wohin geht der Wanderer?

2. Was für ein Wetter ist es?

3. Wie sieht das Wasser aus?

4. Wie reagiert der Wanderer auf die Hitze?

5. Was macht der Fisch?

6. Warum ist der Wanderer allein?

7. Wie fühlt sich das Wasser an?

8. Wie fühlt sich der Wanderer nach dem Schwimmen?

9. Zu welcher Tageszeit wacht der Wanderer auf?

Comprehension Questions

1. Where is the walker going?

2. What kind of weather is it?

3. What does the water look like?

4. How does the walker react to the heat?

5. What is the fish doing?

6. Why is the walker alone?

7. How does the water feel?

8. How does the walker feel after swimming?

9. What time of day is it when the walker wakes up?

Das Haus

Letzte Woche bin ich in mein neues Haus eingezogen, und ich bin so **aufgeregt**! Es ist viel größer als mein altes, und es hat einen großen Garten. Ich kann es kaum erwarten, Freunde zum Grillen und für Partys einzuladen. Mein Lieblingsteil ist mein neues Schlafzimmer. Es ist so groß und hell, und ich habe jede Menge Platz, um all meine Sachen unterzubringen. Ich bin wirklich glücklich mit meinem neuen Haus und denke, dass ich hier sehr glücklich sein werde. Ich beschloss, das Haus noch ein bisschen zu erkunden. Ich ging nach oben in den zweiten Stock und machte mich auf den Weg in die Küche, als ich eine große schwarze Spinne an der Wand sah! Ich schrie auf und rannte die Treppe hinunter. Ich war so **erschrocken**! Aber nach ein paar Minuten beruhigte ich mich und beschloss, wieder nach oben zu gehen. Langsam machte ich mich auf den Weg in die Küche und sah, dass die Spinne weg war. Ich war so erleichtert! Ich ging wieder nach unten und beschloss, nach draußen zu gehen, um den **Garten zu** erkunden. Sie war so groß! Ich konnte es nicht glauben. Ich sah eine Schaukel in der Ecke und eine Rutsche. Ich sah auch ein Basketballnetz und ein **Trampolin**. Ich war so aufgeregt!

Ich kann es kaum erwarten, all diese neuen Sachen zu benutzen. Die **Nachbarn** kamen vorbei und stellten sich vor. Sie schienen wirklich nett zu sein, und wir unterhielten uns eine Weile. Sie luden mich zu ihrem

The House

I moved into my new house last week, and I am so **excited**! It is so much bigger than my old one, and it has a big backyard. I can't wait to have friends over for BBQs and parties. My **favourite** part is my new bedroom. It is so big and bright, and I have lots of space to put all of my things. I am really happy with my new house and I think I will be very happy here. I decided to explore the house a bit more. I went upstairs to the second floor and started making my way to the kitchen when I saw a big black spider on the wall! I screamed and ran downstairs. I was so **scared**! But after a few minutes, I calmed down and decided to go back upstairs. I slowly made my way to the kitchen and saw that the spider was gone. I was so relieved! I went back downstairs and decided to go outside to explore the **backyard**. It was so big! I couldn't believe it. I saw a swing set in the corner and a slide. I also saw a basketball net and a **trampoline**. I was so excited!

I can't wait to use all of this new stuff. The **neighbours** came over and introduced themselves. They seemed really nice, and we talked for a while. They invited me to their BBQ next weekend, and I said I would love to come. I had a great first week in my new house, and I am excited about all of the new adventures that are ahead. Today, I am going to go exploring in the backyard again and see what else I can find. Who knows, maybe I'll even find some **treasure**. I can't wait to see what the next week brings! The next week, I went exploring in the backyard again, and I found a

Grillfest am nächsten Wochenende ein, und ich sagte, dass ich gerne kommen würde. Ich hatte eine tolle erste Woche in meinem neuen Haus und freue mich auf all die neuen Abenteuer, die vor mir liegen. Heute werde ich wieder im Garten auf Entdeckungstour gehen und sehen, was ich noch alles finden kann. Wer weiß, vielleicht finde ich ja sogar einen **Schatz**. Ich kann es kaum erwarten, zu sehen, was die nächste Woche bringt! In der nächsten Woche bin ich wieder im Garten auf Entdeckungsreise gegangen und habe einen **geheimen** Garten gefunden. Er war so schön! Überall waren Blumen und ein kleiner Teich mit Fischen drin. Ich habe auch eine Schaukel gesehen, die ich vorher noch nie gesehen hatte. Ich war so aufgeregt, diesen geheimen Garten zu finden, und ich kann es kaum erwarten, ihn weiter zu erkunden. Er war so **schön**!

Überall gab es Blumen und einen kleinen Teich mit Fischen darin. Ich habe auch eine **Schaukel** gesehen, die ich vorher noch nie gesehen hatte. Ich war so aufgeregt, diesen geheimen Garten zu finden, und ich kann es kaum erwarten, ihn weiter zu erkunden. Mein neues Zimmer hat mir auch gut gefallen. Es war so groß und hell, und an den Wänden hingen bereits Poster von meinen Lieblingsbands. Ich musste nicht einmal meine eigenen **Möbel** mitbringen, denn es gab bereits ein Bett, eine Kommode und einen Schreibtisch. Das wird das beste Jahr aller Zeiten! Ich war ein bisschen nervös, weil ich an einer neuen **Schule** anfing, aber alle meine neuen Nachbarn waren so freundlich.

secret garden. It was so beautiful! There were flowers everywhere and a little pond with fish in it. I also saw a swing set that I hadn't seen before. I was so excited to find this secret garden, and I can't wait to explore it more. It was so **beautiful**!

There were flowers everywhere and a little pond with fish in it. I also saw a **swing** set that I hadn't seen before. I was so excited to find this secret garden, and I can't wait to explore it more. I also loved my new room. It was so big and bright, and there were already posters of my favourite bands on the walls. I didn't even have to bring any of my own **furniture** because there was already a bed, dresser, and desk here. This is going to be the best year ever! I was a little nervous about starting at a new **school**, but all of my new neighbours have been so friendly.

Verständnisfragen

1. Wo wohnt die Person?

2. Wie gefällt es der Person im neuen Haus?

3. Was gefällt der Person am besten an ihrem neuen Haus?

4. Was hat die Person im Garten gefunden?

5. Wer sind die Nachbarn?

6. Wie hat sich die Person in den ersten Tagen in der neuen Wohnung gefühlt?

7. Was gefällt der Person am besten an ihrem neuen Zimmer?

8. Was plant die Person morgen zu tun?

9. Was war das Beste an der ersten Woche im neuen Haus?

10. Was befindet sich alles in dem neuen Zimmer der Person?

Comprehension Questions

1. Where does the person live?

2. How does the person like it in the new house?

3. What is the person's favorite part of the new house?

4. What did the person find in the garden?

5. Who are the neighbors?

6. How did the person's first days in the new house feel?

7. What is the person's favorite part of the new room?

8. What is the person planning to do tomorrow?

9. What was the best part of the person's first week in the new house?

10. What is everything in the person's new room?

Im Zug

Ich rannte zum Bahnhof, aber ich war zu spät. Der Zug war bereits ohne mich abgefahren. Ich war so **wütend** und **enttäuscht** von mir selbst. Ich hatte geplant, mit dem Zug meine Großeltern zu besuchen, die auf dem Land leben, aber jetzt würde ich eine ganze Stunde auf den nächsten Zug warten müssen. Ich beschloss, stattdessen eine Weile durch die Stadt zu laufen und versuchte, die verpasste Gelegenheit zu vergessen. Beim Spazierengehen begann ich von all den Orten zu **träumen, an die man mit dem Zug** gelangen kann. Plötzlich war ich nicht mehr so verärgert. Ich gehe zurück in den Bahnhof und kann nicht umhin, die große rot-weiß-blaue Lokomotive zu bemerken, die auf mich zu tuckert. Erst als ich den **Schaffner** sehe, der mir aus dem Fenster zuwinkt, wird mir klar, dass dieser Zug für mich bestimmt ist. Ich steige ein, suche mir einen Platz und mache mich auf eine lange Reise gefasst.

Als wir aus dem Bahnhof fahren, frage ich mich, wohin dieser Zug mich wohl bringen wird. Durch grüne **Felder** und über blaue Flüsse, vorbei an Bergen und Tälern - man weiß nie, wohin dieser alte Zug fahren wird. Als die Nacht hereinbricht, falle ich in einen **friedlichen** Schlaf, der durch die **rhythmische** Bewegung der Waggons auf den Gleisen unter mir eingelullt wird. Als ich am nächsten Morgen die Augen öffne, sehe ich, dass wir in einer kleinen Stadt irgendwo im Nirgendwo angekommen sind. Die Sonne lugt gerade über den Horizont, als die Einheimischen beginnen, sich auf der

On the train

I ran to the train station, but I was too late. The train had already left without me. I felt so **angry** and **disappointed** with myself. I had been planning to take the train to visit my grandparents who live in the country, but now I would have to wait a whole hour for the next train. I decided to walk around the city for a while instead and tried to forget about my missed opportunity. As I walked, I started **daydreaming** about all of the places that **trains** can take you. Suddenly, I wasn't so upset anymore. I head back into the station and can't help but to notice the large red, white, and blue locomotive chugging its way towards me. It's not until I see the **conductor** waving at me from the window that I realise that this train is for me. I board the train and find my seat, settling in for what promises to be a long journey.

As we pull out of the station, I can't help but wonder where this train will take me. Through **fields** of green and over rivers blue, past mountains and valleys too, there's no telling where this old train will go. As night begins to fall, I drift off into a **peaceful** sleep, lulled by the **rhythmic** movement of the cars on the tracks below. When morning comes again, I open my eyes to find that we've arrived in a small town somewhere in the middle of nowhere. The sun is just peeking over the horizon as locals start milling about on Main Street; it looks like any other day here except for one thing-there's a big sign posted near City Hall that reads "Welcome aboard!" It seems this little town

Hauptstraße zu bewegen. Es sieht aus wie jeder andere Tag hier, bis auf eine Ausnahme: In der Nähe des Rathauses hängt ein großes Schild mit der Aufschrift "Willkommen an Bord! Es scheint, als hätte diese kleine Stadt uns erwartet, obwohl wir nur ein gewöhnlicher Personenzug sind, der auf dem Weg zu einem anderen Ziel durchfährt. Als wir die Stadt wieder hinter uns lassen und in Richtung wer weiß wohin tuckern, lächle ich über all die freundlichen Gesichter, die uns aus den kleinen Häusern zwischen den **Feldern** zuwinken - **es ist** wirklich erstaunlich, wie etwas so scheinbar Alltägliches so viel Freude bereiten kann, wenn man einfach durchfährt. Und dann sind da natürlich noch die **Kinder**.

Ich lehne mich aus dem Fenster meiner Lokomotive. Mit ihren leuchtenden Augen und ihrem breiten Grinsen machen sie mich immer so glücklich. Ich winke ihnen energisch zu, bevor ich in mein **Abteil** zurückkehre und mich setze. Es war schon ein langer Tag, aber er ist noch nicht zu Ende; es sind noch ein paar Stunden, bis wir unser endgültiges **Ziel** erreichen. Ich ziehe mein Buch heraus und beginne zu lesen, während mich das rhythmische Schaukeln des Zuges in einen friedlichen Zustand versetzt. Ab und zu werfe ich einen Blick auf die Landschaft, die draußen vorbeizieht - es wird nie langweilig, egal wie oft ich sie sehe. Schließlich bricht die Nacht herein, und in der Ferne tauchen **funkelnde** Lichter auf; wir nähern uns dem Ziel. Bald darauf fahren wir in den Bahnhof ein und kommen zum Stehen.

has been expecting us, even though we're just an ordinary **passenger** train passing through on our way elsewhere. As we leave town behind us once more, chugging along towards who knows where next, I smile at all the friendly faces waving goodbye from those little houses nestled amongst **farmland**—it really is amazing how something so seemingly ordinary can bring so much joy simply by passing through. And then, of course, there are the **children**.

I lean out the window of my locomotive. They always make me feel so happy with their shining eyes and big grins. I waved back at them energetically before returning to my **cabin** and taking a seat. It's been a long day already, but it's not over yet; there's still another few hours until we reach our final **destination**. I pull out my book and start reading, letting the rhythmic rocking of the train lull me into a peaceful state. Every now and then I glance up at the scenery passing by outside— it never gets old no matter how many times I see it. Eventually, night starts to fall and **twinkling** lights start to appear in the distance; we're getting close now. Soon enough, we're pulling into the station and coming to a stop.

Verständnisfragen

1. Wohin fährt der Zug?

2. Wer reist mit dem Zug?

3. Wann fährt der Zug ab?

4. Wie kommt der Protagonist in den Zug?

5. Woher kommt der Zug?

6. Wohin fährt der Zug als nächstes?

7. Wann sind die Passagiere angekommen?

8. Wie fühlt sich der Protagonist, als er den Zug verpasst?

9. Wie reagiert der Zugführer, als er den Protagonisten sieht?

Comprehension Questions

1. Where is the train going?

2. Who is traveling on the train?

3. When does the train leave?

4. How does the protagonist get on the train?

5. Where does the train come from?

6. Where is the train going next?

7. When did the passengers arrive?

8. How does the protagonist feel when he misses the train?

9. How does the train driver react when he sees the protagonist?

Abendessen kochen

Es ist jetzt 17 Uhr und ich gehe von der Arbeit nach Hause. Ich freue **mich** auf einen ruhigen Abend zu Hause mit meinem Partner. Wir werden gemeinsam kochen und uns dann den Rest des Abends entspannen. Es ist ein gutes Gefühl, zu wissen, dass ich heute **Abend** keine Pläne oder Verpflichtungen habe. Als ich zu Hause ankomme, steht mein Partner bereits in der Küche und beginnt mit der Zubereitung unseres Abendessens. Es riecht **fantastisch** hier drin! Während wir kochen, plaudern wir über den Tag des anderen und erzählen uns kleine Geschichten aus unserem Arbeitsleben. Die Küche ist mein Lieblingsraum in unserer Wohnung. Ich liebe es zu kochen, und ganz besonders liebe ich es, mit meinem Partner zu kochen. Wir haben immer so viel Spaß hier drin, lachen und scherzen, während wir kochen. Außerdem ist das Essen immer **unglaublich**, wenn wir **zusammen** arbeiten.

Heute Abend machen wir eines meiner absoluten Lieblingsrezepte: **Hähnchen** Parmesan. Mein Partner beginnt mit dem Panieren des Hähnchens, während ich die Soße auf dem **Herd** zum Kochen bringe. Wir arbeiten zusammen wie eine gut geölte Maschine, und schon bald ist das Abendessen servierfertig. Wir setzen uns an unseren kleinen Küchentisch mit **Tellern voller** Hähnchen Parmesan, Nudeln und Salat. Wir stoßen mit den Gläsern an und nehmen unseren ersten Bissen - und der ist **himmlisch**! Das Hähnchen ist

Cooking Dinner

It's 5 pm now and I am walking home from work. I'm looking **forward** to having a calm evening at home with my partner. We'll cook dinner together and then just relax for the rest of the night. It feels good to know that I don't have any plans or obligations this **evening**. I arrive home and my partner is already in the kitchen, starting to prepare our dinner. It smells **amazing** in here! We chat as we cook, catching up on each other's days and sharing little stories from our work lives. The kitchen is my favourite room in our apartment. I love cooking, and I especially love cooking with my partner. We always have such a good time in here, laughing and joking around while we cook up a storm. Plus, the food is always **incredible** when we work **together**.

Tonight, we're making one of my all-time favourite recipes: **chicken** Parmesan. My partner starts by breading the chicken while I get the sauce simmering on the **stovetop**. We work together like a well-oiled machine, and before long, dinner is ready to serve. We sit down at our little kitchen table with **plates** heaped high with chicken Parmesan, pasta, and salad. We clink glasses and take our first bite—and it's **heavenly**! The chicken is crispy on the outside but juicy on the inside; the sauce is flavorful and perfect; the pasta is cooked al dente... everything tastes absolutely perfect tonight. We both know that this was one of those nights where everything just came together perfectly as we **savour** every last bite of our delicious meal. It tasted even better than it smelled—which was pretty damn good!

außen knusprig, aber innen saftig; die Soße ist würzig und perfekt; die Nudeln sind al dente gekocht... alles schmeckt heute Abend absolut perfekt. Wir wissen beide, dass dies einer dieser Abende war, an denen alles perfekt zusammenpasst, und wir **genießen** jeden einzelnen Bissen unseres köstlichen Essens. Es hat sogar noch besser geschmeckt, als es gerochen hat - und das war verdammt gut! Wir sind relativ schnell fertig mit dem Essen, da keiner von uns heute besonders hungrig ist, aber wir lassen uns Zeit und genießen noch ein paar **Gläser** Wein, während wir uns über dieses und jenes Thema unterhalten. Nach dem Essen räumen wir schnell zusammen auf und gehen dann ins Wohnzimmer, wo wir noch eine Weile auf der Couch **kuscheln** und fernsehen.

Es ist so schön, sich nach einem langen **Arbeitstag** einfach nur nahe zu sein. Ich fühle mich zufrieden. Auch wenn wir keinen ereignisreichen Abend hatten, war es schön, einfach etwas Zeit miteinander zu verbringen, ohne das Haus verlassen zu müssen. Wir haben uns einen Film angesehen und sind früh ins Bett gegangen, weil wir mit unserem einfachen Abend **zufrieden waren**. Das ist zu einer unserer **Lieblingsbeschäftigungen** an Abenden geworden, an denen wir nicht ausgehen wollen - einfach zu Hause entspannen und die Gesellschaft des anderen bei einem selbstgekochten Essen genießen. Es ist immer schön zu wissen, dass wir nach einem langen Tag hierher zurückkommen und einfach wir selbst sein können.

We finish our meal relatively quickly as neither of us is particularly hungry today, but we take our time enjoying a few more **glasses** of wine while chatting lightly about this and that topic. After dinner, we clean up quickly together and then move into the living room, where we spend some time **cuddling** on the couch while watching TV.

It feels so nice just being close to each other after a long day apart **working**. I feel content. Even though we didn't have an eventful evening, it was nice to just spend some time together without having to leave the house. We watched a movie and went to bed early, feeling **satisfied** with our simple night in. This has become one of our **favourite** things to do on nights when we don't want to go out—just relax at home and enjoy each other's company over a home-cooked meal. It's always nice to know that we can come back here after a long day and just be ourselves.

Verständnisfragen

1. Woher kommt der Erzähler?

2. Was macht der Erzähler nach der Arbeit?

3. Was isst der Erzähler zum Abendessen?

4. Warum mag der Erzähler die Küche?

5. Was für ein Gericht kocht das Paar?

6. Wie fühlt sich der Erzähler am Ende des Abends?

7. Was ist die Lieblingsbeschäftigung des Paares?

8. Was tun die beiden, wenn sie müde werden?

9. Wo schlafen sie?

10. Warum bleibt der Erzähler gerne zu Hause?

Comprehension Questions

1. Where does the narrator come from?

2. What does the narrator do after work?

3. What does the narrator eat for dinner?

4. Why does the narrator like the kitchen?

5. What kind of dish does the couple cook?

6. How does the narrator feel at the end of the evening?

7. What is the couple's favorite thing to do?

8. What do the couple do when they get tired?

9. Where do they sleep?

10. Why does the narrator like to stay at home?

Nach Hause gehen

Es war eine **friedliche** Nacht, als ich von der Arbeit nach Hause ging. Als ich ging, konnte ich nicht anders, als über die Erinnerungen zu lächeln. Es fühlte sich gut an, wieder in meiner alten Nachbarschaft zu sein. Ich winkte ein paar Leuten zu, die ich kannte, und sie winkten zurück. Es war schön, wieder zu Hause zu sein. Ich ging an meiner alten Schule vorbei und **erinnerte mich an** all die guten Zeiten, die ich mit meinen Freunden hatte. Wir gingen immer zusammen nach Hause und sprachen über unseren Tag. **Manchmal hielten** wir an, um ein Eis zu essen oder in den Park zu gehen. Das waren die besten Zeiten. Ich vermisse diese Zeiten. Aber jetzt habe ich meine eigene Familie und bin glücklich mit meinem Leben. Ich bin froh, dass ich auf diese Erinnerungen zurückblicken und lächeln kann. Sie sind ein Teil meines Lebens, den ich immer in Ehren halten werde. Das waren die besten Zeiten. Ich vermisse diese Zeiten. Aber jetzt habe ich meine eigene Familie und bin glücklich mit meinem Leben. Ich bin froh, dass ich auf diese **Erinnerungen** zurückblicken und lächeln kann. Sie sind ein Teil meines Lebens, den ich immer in Ehren halten werde.

Ich gehe weiter und denke an die schöne Zeit, die ich mit meinen Freunden hatte. Ich weiß, dass ich sie bald wiedersehen werde. Ich mache mich auf den Weg nach Hause und beschließe, durch einen nahe gelegenen Park zu gehen. Die Sonne geht gerade unter und der Himmel färbt sich in ein **schönes** Orange. Der Park ist leer, bis auf ein paar Vögel, die in den Bäumen

Walking Home

It was a **peaceful** night as I walked home from work. As I walked, I couldn't help but smile at the memories. It felt good to be back in my old neighborhood. I waved to a few people I knew, and they waved back. It was good to be home. I walked past my old school and **remembered** all the good times I had with my friends. We would always walk home together and talk about our day. **Sometimes** we would stop and get ice cream or go to the park. Those were the best times. I miss those times. But now I have my own family and I'm happy with my life. I'm glad I can look back on those memories and smile. They are a part of my life that I will always cherish. Those were the best times. I miss those times. But now I have my own family and I'm happy with my life. I'm glad I can look back on those **memories** and smile. They are a part of my life that I will always cherish.

I keep walking, thinking about the good times I had with my friends. I know I'll see them again soon. I head towards my home and decide to walk through a park nearby. The sun is setting and the sky is turning a **beautiful** orange color. The park is empty, except for a few birds chirping in the trees. I take a deep **breath** and smile. As I walk through the park, I see a shooting star streak across the sky. I made a wish on that star, and kept walking. I think about my day at work and how **peaceful** it was. I smile to myself, thinking about how lucky I am to have such a great job. I walk home,

zwitschern. Ich **atme** tief ein und lächle. Als ich durch den Park gehe, sehe ich eine Sternschnuppe über den Himmel huschen. Ich wünsche mir etwas von dieser Sternschnuppe und laufe weiter. Ich denke an meinen Arbeitstag und daran, wie **friedlich** er war. Ich lächle vor mich hin und denke daran, wie viel Glück ich habe, einen so tollen Job zu haben. Ich gehe nach Hause und **spüre** die kühle Nachtluft auf meiner Haut. Ich fühle mich so lebendig und glücklich, weil ich es einfach genieße, in einer friedlichen Nacht nach Hause zu gehen.

Ich fühlte mich so gut, dass ich anfing zu **pfeifen**. Ich ging an ein paar Leuten auf der Straße vorbei, aber sie kümmerten sich alle um ihre eigenen Angelegenheiten.

Ich bog um die Ecke in meine Straße und sah den Kater meines Nachbarn, Mr. Whiskers, auf meiner Veranda sitzen. Ich grüßte ihn, und er miaute zurück. Ich **schloss** meine Tür auf und ging hinein. Ich war so froh, zu Hause zu sein. Ich zog meine Schuhe aus und machte mich bettfertig. Ich ging an diesem Abend mit einem Gefühl der Freude und Dankbarkeit ins Bett, mein Herz war voller Liebe. Ich schlief die ganze Nacht durch und machte mir keine Sorgen. Ich wachte aus einem erholsamen Schlaf auf und wurde von der Sonne **begrüßt**, die durch mein Fenster hereinschien. Ich stand auf und streckte mich, atmete tief ein und spürte, wie die kühle Luft meine Lungen füllte. Ich ging zu meinem Fenster und schaute hinaus, hörte die Vögel zwitschern und die **Eichhörnchen** spielen.

feeling the cool night air on my skin. I feel so alive and happy, just enjoying the simple act of walking home on a peaceful night.
I felt so good, I started **whistling**. I walked past a few people on the street, but they were all minding their own business.

I turned the corner onto my street and saw my neighbor's cat, Mr. Whiskers, sitting on my porch. I said hello to him and he meowed back. I **unlocked** my door and went inside. I was so happy to be home. I took off my shoes and got ready for bed. I went to bed that night feeling happy and grateful, my heart full of love. I slept soundly through the night, not worrying about anything. I woke up from a restful sleep and was **greeted** by the sun shining in through my window. I got out of bed and stretched, taking a deep breath and feeling the cool air fill my lungs. I walked to my window and looked out, hearing the birds chirping and the **squirrels** playing.

Verständnisfragen

1. Was machte der Protagonist, als die Geschichte begann?

2. Woran hat der Protagonist auf dem Heimweg gedacht?

3. Was hat der Protagonist nach der Schule mit seinen Freunden gemacht?

4. Was vermisst der Protagonist aus dieser Zeit?

5. Was denkt der Protagonist über sein gegenwärtiges Leben?

6. Was tut der Protagonist, wenn er eine Sternschnuppe sieht?

7. Wie fühlt sich der Protagonist, wenn er nach Hause geht?

8. Was macht der Protagonist, wenn er nach Hause kommt?

9. Wie fühlt sich der Protagonist, wenn er am nächsten Morgen aufwacht?

Comprehension Questions

1. What was the protagonist doing when the story started?

2. What did the protagonist think about when walking home?

3. What did the protagonist used to do with friends after school?

4. What does the protagonist miss about those times?

5. What does the protagonist think about their current life?

6. What does the protagonist do when they see a shooting star?

7. How does the protagonist feel when they walk home?

8. What does the protagonist do when they get home?

9. How does the protagonist feel when they wake up the next morning?

Das Schloss

Die Familie wollte schon immer ein altes Schloss in **Deutschland** besichtigen, und schließlich machten sie sich auf den Weg. Sie wurden nicht **enttäuscht**. Das Schloss war wunderschön, und sie genossen es, die vielen Räume und Gänge zu erkunden. Das erste, was ihnen auffiel, war der Geruch. Sie fanden **Schimmel**, Feuchtigkeit und etwas anderes, das sie nicht genau zuordnen konnten. Das zweite war der Klang. Steinmauern sind zwar dick, aber sie dämpfen den Schall nicht vollständig. Sie hörten jeden Schritt, jedes Wort, das mit normaler Stimme gesprochen wurde, und das gelegentliche Tröpfeln von Wasser **irgendwo** in der Ferne. Als sich ihre Augen an das schwache Licht gewöhnt hatten, sahen sie um sich herum massive Steinwände, an denen Wandteppiche in **Fetzen** hingen. Sie befanden sich in einer riesigen Halle mit einer hohen Decke, die von geschnitzten Säulen getragen wurde. Auch die Aussicht von den Türmen gefiel ihnen, und die Kinder hatten viel Spaß beim Herumtollen auf dem Gelände. Als sie mit der Erkundung des Schlosses fertig waren, ging die **Sonne** bereits unter, und sie bedauerten, dass sie keine **Taschenlampe** mitgenommen hatten. Sie beschlossen, sich auf den Rückweg zum Eingang zu machen, aber sie hatten sich bald verlaufen. Sie irrten gefühlte Stunden umher, bis sie schließlich auf eine Tür stießen, die nach draußen führte. Sie gingen weiter, bis sie das Ende des Flurs **erreichten** und vor einer imposanten Doppeltür standen. So sehr sie sich auch bemühten, die Türen

The castle

The family had always wanted to visit an old castle in **Germany**, and finally they took the trip. They were not **disappointed**. The castle was beautiful, and they enjoyed exploring its many rooms and corridors. The first thing that hit them was the smell. They found **mould**, dampness, and something else they couldn't quite put their finger on. The second thing was the sound. Stone walls are thick, but they don't deaden sound completely. They heard every footstep, every word spoken in a normal voice, and the occasional drip of water **somewhere** in the distance. As their eyes adjusted to the dim light, they saw massive stone walls looming all around them, tapestries hanging from them in **tattered** shreds. They were standing in a huge hall with a high ceiling supported by carved pillars. They also loved the views from the turrets, and the kids had a great time running around the grounds. The **sun** had begun to set by the time they finished exploring the castle, and they regretted that they hadn't brought a **flashlight**. They decided to make their way back to the entrance, but soon found themselves lost. They wandered around for what felt like hours, until finally they came across a door that led outside. They continued until they **reached** the end of the hall and came to an imposing set of double doors. Try as they might, the doors wouldn't budge. They rattle **ominously** but don't move an inch. It looked like whoever was here before must have gone through here and locked them from inside. Eventually, they find a way out. Relief washed over them as they stepped out into the cool

rührten sich nicht. Sie klapperten **bedrohlich**, aber sie bewegten sich keinen Zentimeter. Es sah so aus, als ob derjenige, der vorher hier war, hier durchgegangen sein musste und sie von innen verriegelt hatte. Schließlich fanden sie einen Weg nach draußen. Erleichterung überkam sie, als sie in die kühle Nachtluft hinaustraten.

Die Sonne begann unterzugehen, und sie **bedauerten,** dass sie keine Taschenlampe mitgenommen hatten. Sie beschlossen, sich auf den Weg zurück zum Eingang zu machen, aber sie hatten sich bald verlaufen. Sie irrten gefühlte Stunden umher, bis sie schließlich auf eine Tür stießen, die **nach draußen** führte. Erleichterung machte sich in ihnen breit, als sie in die kühle Nachtluft hinaustraten. Am nächsten Abend nahmen sie auf jeden Fall eine Taschenlampe mit, um den Rest des Schlosses zu erkunden. Sie gingen durch den **Innenhof** und hinunter zum Fluss, der hinter den Schlossmauern verlief. Als sie umhergingen, hörten sie seltsame Geräusche. Es klang, als würde sie jemand verfolgen. Sie beschleunigten ihren Schritt, aber die Geräusche wurden lauter und kamen näher. Die Familie rannte so schnell sie konnte zum Schloss zurück und war erleichtert, dass die Gestalt in dem **dunklen** Mantel ihnen nicht gefolgt war.

Sie gingen zurück in ihr Zimmer und versuchten zu vergessen, was geschehen war, aber sie wurden das Gefühl nicht los, dass sie von etwas aus dem Schatten beobachtet wurden. Als sie drinnen waren, **verbarrikadierten** sie die Türen und Fenster und riefen die Polizei.

night air.

The sun had begun to set, and they **regretted** that they hadn't brought a flashlight. They decided to make their way back to the entrance, but soon found themselves lost. They wandered around for what felt like hours, until finally they came across a door that led **outside**. Relief washed over them as they stepped out into the cool night air. The next evening, they made sure to take a flashlight with them as they explored the rest of the castle. They walked through the **courtyard** and down to the river that ran behind the **castle** walls. As they walked around, they began to hear strange noises. It sounded like someone was following them. They quickened their pace, but the noises got louder and closer. The family ran back to the castle as fast as they could, and they were relieved to see that the figure in the **dark** cloak had not followed them.

They went back to their room and tried to forget about what had happened, but they could not shake the feeling that something was watching them from the shadows. Once they were inside, they **barricaded** the doors and windows and called the police.

Verständnisfragen

1. Was hat die Familie getan, als sie sich im Schloss verlaufen hat?

2. Wie hat sich die Familie gefühlt, als sie erfuhr, dass es sich nur um einen Einheimischen handelte?

3. Was hat der Mann getan, dass man ihn verhaftet hat?

4. Wie lautete das Urteil für den Mann?

5. Welches Geräusch hat die Familie gehört, während sie spazieren ging?

6. Wo war die Gestalt in dem dunklen Mantel, als die Familie sie sah?

7. Was hat die Familie getan, als sie in ihr Zimmer zurückkam?

8. Wann hat die Familie das Schloss wieder erkundet?

9. Was war das, was die Familie nicht ausmachen konnte?

Comprehension Questions

1. What did the family do when they got lost in the castle?

2. How did the family feel when they found out it was just a local man?

3. What did the man do that got him arrested?

4. What was the sentence for the man?

5. What noise did the family hear while they were walking?

6. Where was the figure in the dark cloak when the family saw him?

7. What did the family do when they got back to their room?

8. When did the family go explore the castle again?

9. What was the thing the family could not make out?

Mein Garten

Mein Garten ist mein Lieblingsplatz. Ich gehe jeden Tag hinaus, egal ob es regnet oder scheint, und verbringe Zeit damit, meine Pflanzen zu pflegen. Ich habe von **allem ein** bisschen - **Gemüse**, Obst, Blumen, Kräuter. Ich habe sogar ein paar Hühner, die mir helfen, die Schädlinge in Schach zu halten. Ich beginne meine Tage im Garten, indem ich den Hühnern Eier abhole. Dann schaue ich nach meinem Gemüse und stelle sicher, dass es genug Wasser und Sonne bekommt. Ich jäte Unkraut auf den Beeten und entferne Ungeziefer, das die Pflanzen **angreifen** könnte. Wenn **alles erledigt** ist, lehne ich mich zurück und genieße den Frieden und die Ruhe der Natur.

Ich habe schon immer gerne Zeit in meinem Garten verbracht. Es hat etwas, von der Natur und all der **Schönheit**, die sie zu bieten hat, umgeben zu sein. Ich empfinde ihn als einen sehr friedlichen und beruhigenden Ort. Ich verbringe oft Zeit in meinem Garten, um mich zu entspannen und die Landschaft zu genießen. Ich arbeite auch gerne in meinem Garten und baue Dinge an. Ich habe einen ziemlich großen Garten, in dem ich gerne **verschiedene** Dinge anbaue. Ich baue Blumen, **Gemüse** und Kräuter an. Ich habe auch ein paar Obstbäume, die leckere Äpfel, Birnen und Pflaumen hervorbringen. Ich baue nicht nur Dinge an, sondern verbringe auch gerne Zeit damit, durch meinen Garten zu spazieren und all die verschiedenen Pflanzen und Tiere zu **bewundern**, die dort zu Hause sind. Im Laufe der Jahre habe ich viele Stunden damit

My Garden

My garden is my happy place. I go out there every day, rain or shine, and spend time tending to my plants. I have a little bit of **everything**-vegetables, fruits, flowers, herbs. I even have a few chickens that help keep the pests at bay. I start my days in the garden by gathering eggs from the chickens. Then I check on my veggies, making sure they are getting enough water and sun. I weed the beds and pick off any bugs that might be **attacking** the plants. Once **everything** is taken care of, I sit back and enjoy the peace and quiet of nature.

I have always loved spending time in my garden. There is something about being surrounded by nature and all of the **beauty** that it has to offer. I find it to be a very peaceful and calming place. I often spend time in my garden just relaxing and enjoying the scenery. I also enjoy working in my garden and growing things. I have a pretty good-sized garden, and I like to grow a variety of **different** things in it. I grow flowers, **vegetables**, and herbs. I also have a few fruit trees that produce some delicious apples, pears, and plums. In addition to growing things, I also enjoy spending time just walking around my garden, **admiring** all of the different plants and animals that call it home. I have spent many hours over the years working on making my **garden** into a place that is not only beautiful but also functional. I love to watch the birds flit around and listen to them sing. Sometimes I even bring out a book and read in the garden while surrounded by all the beauty that I've created. **Gardening** is my passion and it brings me so

verbracht, meinen **Garten** zu einem Ort zu machen, der nicht nur schön, sondern auch funktional ist. Ich liebe es, den Vögeln beim Herumfliegen zuzusehen und ihnen beim Singen zuzuhören. Manchmal nehme ich sogar ein Buch mit und lese im Garten, während ich von all der Schönheit umgeben bin, die ich geschaffen habe. **Gartenarbeit** ist meine Leidenschaft und bringt mir so viel Freude. Jeder Tag in meinem Garten ist ein guter Tag.

Eine meiner Lieblingsbeschäftigungen ist das Kochen, daher ist ein gut bestückter Kräutergarten für mich sehr **wichtig**. Thymian, Basilikum, Oregano, Rosmarin, Salbei und Lavendel sind nur einige der Kräuter, die ich gerne in meinem Garten anbaue, damit ich sie beim Kochen für mich oder für **Gäste** verwenden kann. Ein weiterer wichtiger Punkt in meinem Garten ist, dass er viel Farbe hat. Um dieses Ziel zu erreichen, baue ich eine Vielzahl von Blumen an, darunter **Rosen**, Lilien, Gänseblümchen, Tulpen, Impatiens, Ringelblumen, usw. Zusätzlich zu den Blumen, die für Farbe sorgen, verwende ich auch gerne verschiedene **Texturen** im Garten, um ihn interessanter zu gestalten. So pflanze ich zum Beispiel Farne neben hoch aufragenden Sonnenblumen oder Hosta **neben** stacheligen Ziergräsern. Ganz gleich, was sonst im Leben passiert, bei der Arbeit in meinem Garten fühle ich mich immer mehr mit der Natur verbunden und mit mir selbst im Reinen.

much joy. Every day in my garden is a good day.

One of the things that I love to do is cook, so having a well-stocked herb garden is very **important** to me. Thyme, basil, oregano, rosemary, sage, and lavender are just some of the herbs that I like to grow in my garden so that I can use them when cooking meals for myself or for **guests**. Another thing that is important to me when it comes to my garden is making sure that there is plenty of colour throughout it. To achieve this goal, I grow a wide variety of flowers, including **roses**, lilies, daisies, tulips, impatiens, marigolds, etc. In addition to adding colour with flowers, I also like to add interest by using different **textures** throughout the garden. For instance, I might plant ferns beneath towering sunflowers or hostas **alongside** spiky ornamental grasses. No matter what else might be going on in life, working in my garden always **manages** to help me feel more connected to nature and at peace with myself.

Verständnisfragen

1. Wo befindet sich der Garten des Autors?

2. Wie viele Hühner hat der Autor?

3. Was macht der Autor jeden Tag im Garten?

4. Warum gefällt dem Autor der Garten?

5. Welche Kräuter pflanzt der Autor in seinem Garten an?

6. Warum ist es für den Autor wichtig, dass es in seinem Garten viele Farben gibt?

7. Wie bringt der Autor Abwechslung in seinen Garten?

8. Wie fühlt sich der Autor, wenn er in seinem Garten arbeitet?

9. Wodurch fühlt sich der Autor verbunden, wenn er in seinem Garten ist?

10. Warum ist jeder Tag im Garten des Autors ein guter Tag?

Comprehension Questions

1. Where is the author's garden?

2. How many chickens does the author have?

3. What does the author do in the garden every day?

4. Why does the author like the garden?

5. What herbs does the author plant in the garden?

6. Why is it important to the author that there are many colors in his garden?

7. How does the author bring variety to his garden?

8. How does the author feel when he works in his garden?

9. What makes the author feel connected when he is in his garden?

10. Why is every day in the author's garden a good day?

Einkaufen gehen

Ich gehe gerne im Einkaufszentrum einkaufen. Es macht immer so viel Spaß, herumzulaufen und sich all die verschiedenen Geschäfte anzuschauen. Im Einkaufszentrum ist für jeden etwas dabei, und es ist immer ein guter Ort, um Angebote für Kleidung, Schuhe und Accessoires zu finden. **Normalerweise** beginne ich meinen Einkaufsbummel, indem ich durch den **Haupteingang** des Einkaufszentrums gehe. Von dort aus gehe ich zuerst zu meinen Lieblingsgeschäften. Nachdem ich in diesen Geschäften gestöbert habe, laufe ich herum und schaue, ob es in anderen Geschäften Sonderangebote gibt. Normalerweise verbringe ich ein paar Stunden im Einkaufszentrum, bevor ich meine Einkäufe erledige. Ich nehme mir beim Einkaufen immer gerne Zeit**, weil** ich sichergehen will, dass ich **genau** das bekomme, was ich will. Außerdem macht es auf diese Weise einfach mehr Spaß!

Ich finde es immer **faszinierend**, die Leute zu beobachten, wenn ich im Einkaufszentrum bin. An der Art und Weise, wie sie einkaufen, kann man wirklich viel über eine Person erkennen. Manche Leute gehen sehr methodisch vor und lassen sich Zeit, während andere einfach **alles zu** nehmen scheinen, **was sie kriegen** können, und so schnell wie möglich zur Kasse gehen. Es gibt auch Leute, die mehr daran interessiert sind, mit ihrem Handy zu telefonieren oder SMS zu schreiben, als sich die Waren anzusehen! Aber egal, welche Art von Käufer man ist, jeder scheint einen

Going Shopping

I love going **shopping** in the mall. It's always so much fun to walk around and look at all the different stores. There's something for everyone in the mall, and it's always a great place to find deals on clothes, shoes, and accessories. I **usually** start my shopping trip by walking through the main **entrance** of the mall. From there, I head to my favourite stores first. After looking through those stores, I'll walk around and see if there are any sales going on at other places. I usually end up spending a couple hours in the mall before I finally make my purchases. I always like to take my time when shopping **because** I want to make sure that I'm getting **exactly** what I want. Plus, it's just more fun that way!

I always find it so **fascinating** to people watch while I'm at the mall. You can really tell a lot about a person by the way they shop. Some people are very methodical and take their time, while others just seem to grab **whatever** they can and head for the check-out as fast as possible. There are also those shoppers who seem more interested in talking on their cell phones or texting than actually looking at any of the merchandise! No matter what kind of shopper you are, though, everyone seems to enjoy window shopping—even if you don't actually buy anything. There's just something about looking at all of the pretty things in the store **windows** that makes me happy. Sometimes I fantasise about what it would be like if I could afford **everything** I see! All in all, spending a day shopping at the mall is one of my favourite pastimes. It's a great way to relax and

Schaufensterbummel zu genießen - auch wenn man nichts kauft. Der Anblick all der schönen Dinge in den **Schaufenstern** macht mich einfach glücklich. Manchmal stelle ich mir vor, wie es wäre, wenn ich mir **alles, was** ich sehe, leisten könnte! Alles in allem ist ein Einkaufstag im Einkaufszentrum eine meiner Lieblingsbeschäftigungen. Es ist eine tolle Möglichkeit, sich zu entspannen und zu relaxen und sich dabei auch noch ein bisschen zu bewegen (wenn man genug läuft). Außerdem ist es **immer** schön, sich hin und wieder ein neues Hemd oder ein Paar Schuhe zu gönnen!

Ich hatte einen **langen** Arbeitstag und endlich etwas Zeit für mich, also beschloss ich, im Einkaufszentrum einkaufen zu gehen. Ich brauchte ein paar neue Kleider für die **kommende** Saison. Sobald ich das Einkaufszentrum betrat, sah ich all die hellen Lichter und die glänzenden Schaufensterfronten. Ich ging zuerst in mein Lieblingsgeschäft und stöberte durch die Regale. Ich fand ein paar schöne Oberteile und probierte sie in der Umkleidekabine an. Als ich mich im Spiegel betrachtete, hörte ich, wie jemand in die Umkleidekabine neben mir kam. Ich erkannte die Stimme als eine meiner Kolleginnen. Wir begrüßten uns und begannen über die Arbeit zu plaudern. Nach ein paar Minuten waren wir beide fertig und gingen **unserer** Wege, trafen uns dann aber später wieder. Wir unterhielten uns weiter und stellten fest, dass wir mehr gemeinsam hatten, als wir dachten. Wir tranken noch etwas und gingen dann nach Hause, **erschöpft** von einem langen Einkaufstag, aber dennoch zufrieden mit unseren Einkäufen.

unwind while also getting a little bit of exercise (if you walk around enough). Plus, it's **always** nice to treat yourself to a new shirt or pair of shoes every now and then!

I had a **long** day at work and finally had some time to myself, so I decided to go shopping at the mall. I needed some new clothes for the **upcoming** season. As soon as I walked in, I saw all the bright lights and shiny storefronts. I headed to my favourite store first and started browsing through the racks. I found a few cute tops and tried them on in the dressing room. As I was looking at myself in the mirror, I heard someone coming into the **dressing** room next to mine. I recognised their voice as one of my co-workers. We said hello and started chatting about work. After a few minutes, we both finished up and went our **separate** ways, but then ran into each other again later. We continued chatting and realised that we had more in common than we thought. We finished our drinks and then headed home for the night, **exhausted** from a long day of shopping but happy with our purchases nonetheless.

Verständnisfragen

1. Wo lagern Sie am liebsten?

2. Welches ist Ihr Lieblingsgeschäft im Einkaufszentrum?

3. Wie lange bleiben Sie normalerweise im Einkaufszentrum?

4. Was denken Sie über Menschen, die viel Zeit im Einkaufszentrum verbringen? 5. Was machst du am liebsten in einem Einkaufszentrum?

6. Haben Sie schon einmal etwas im Einkaufszentrum gekauft, obwohl Sie es nicht wirklich brauchten?

7. Wie reagieren Sie, wenn Sie im Einkaufszentrum etwas sehen, das Ihnen wirklich gefallen würde, aber zu teuer ist?

8. Haben Sie schon einmal etwas im Einkaufszentrum gesehen und sich gefragt, wer es wohl kaufen würde?

9. Was halten Sie von Leuten, die im Einkaufszentrum mit ihren Handys beschäftigt sind, anstatt sich die Geschäfte anzusehen?

Comprehension Questions

1. Where do you like to store the most?

2. What is your favorite store in the mall?

3. How long do you usually stay at the mall?

4. What do you think about people who spend a lot of time at the mall? 5. what is your favorite thing to do at the mall?

6. Have you ever bought something at the mall when you didn't really need it?

7. How do you react when you see something at the mall that you would really like, but it is too expensive?

8. Have you ever seen something at the mall and wondered who would buy it?

9. What is your opinion about people who are busy with their cell phones in the mall instead of looking at the stores?

Auf dem Markt

Am Samstagmorgen wache ich früh auf und will unbedingt auf den **Markt**, bevor es zu voll wird. Ich ziehe mir etwas an und gehe zur Tür hinaus, wobei ich unterwegs meine wiederverwendbaren Taschen mitnehme. Auf dem Weg dorthin überlege ich, was ich in der kommenden Woche zubereiten möchte. Ich weiß, dass ich mindestens einmal Gemüse **braten** will, also muss ich gutes Gemüse kaufen. Außerdem möchte ich eine Suppe oder einen Eintopf kochen, also muss ich auch etwas Fleisch kaufen. Ich muss sehen, was gut aussieht, wenn ich dort bin. Der Markt ist nur ein paar Häuserblocks entfernt, und ich sehe schon die aufgebauten Stände und die **Menschen, die** sich dort tummeln.

Ich komme auf dem Markt an und steuere direkt auf den Gemüsestand zu. Die Auswahl ist großartig, und ich fülle meine Taschen mit einer Vielzahl von **frischen** Produkten. Ich unterhalte mich ein wenig mit dem Landwirt, und er empfiehlt mir einige Rezepte. Ich bin gespannt darauf, sie auszuprobieren. Beim Einkaufen plaudere ich mit den **Landwirten** und lerne sie und ihre Produkte kennen. Nachdem ich alles Gemüse eingekauft habe, was ich brauche, gehe ich zur Fleischabteilung. Hier bin ich etwas zögerlicher, da ich mir nicht sicher bin, was ich kaufen möchte. Schließlich entscheide ich mich für Hühnerfleisch, weil es vielseitig ist und für eine Vielzahl von Gerichten verwendet werden kann. Ich kaufe auch

At the Market

I wake up early on Saturday morning, eager to get to the **market** before it gets too crowded. I throw on some clothes and head out the door, grabbing my reusable bags on the way. As I walk, I start planning what I want to make for the week ahead. I know I want to **roast** vegetables at least once, so I'll need to buy some good quality vegetables. I also want to make a soup or stew, so I'll need to get some meat as well. I'll have to see what looks good when I get there. The market is only a few blocks away, and I can already see the stalls set up and the **people** milling about.

I arrive at the market and head straight for the vegetable stand. The selection is beautiful, and I fill my bags with a variety of **fresh** produce. I chat with the farmer for a bit, and he recommends some recipes to me. I'm excited to try them out. I chat with the **farmers** as I shop, getting to know them and their products. After I have all the vegetables I need, I move on to the meat section. I'm a bit more hesitant here, as I'm not sure what I want to get. I eventually decide on chicken because it is versatile and can be used in a variety of dishes. I also buy a few different cuts of meat, making sure to get grass-fed beef and free-range **chicken**. The butcher was a friendly man, always cheerful despite the long hours he worked. He wrapped up my chicken breasts and steak before chatting to me about his weekend plans. I said goodbye to him and continued on my way. I also grabbed some eggs and cheese from the

verschiedene Fleischsorten, wobei ich darauf achte, dass ich Rindfleisch aus Weidehaltung und **Huhn** aus Freilandhaltung kaufe. Der Metzger war ein freundlicher Mann, der trotz seiner langen Arbeitszeiten immer gut gelaunt war. Er wickelte meine Hühnerbrust und mein Steak ein und plauderte mit mir über seine Pläne fürs Wochenende. Ich verabschiedete mich von ihm und setzte meinen Weg fort. Ich kaufte auch noch ein paar Eier und Käse aus der Molkereiabteilung.

Auf dem Markt herrschte reges Treiben, und alle wollten die frischen Produkte und das Fleisch, die angeboten wurden, kaufen. Die Luft war dick mit dem Geruch von Knoblauch und Zwiebeln, und das Lachen und die Gespräche erfüllten die Luft. Ich bahnte mir einen Weg durch die Menge und suchte mir die anderen Artikel für meinen Wocheneinkauf aus. Ich füllte meinen **Korb** mit Obst und Gemüse, Nudeln und Brot, bevor ich mich auf den Weg zur Kasse machte. Die Schlange war lang, aber sie bewegte sich schnell. Schließlich waren die letzten **Lebensmittel** eingekauft, und es war Zeit, nach Hause zu fahren. Das Auto wurde beladen, und die Fahrt nach Hause war lang und mühsam. Der Verkehr war dicht, und die Hitze war drückend. Endlich fuhr das Auto in die Einfahrt, und die Erleichterung war spürbar. Das Haus war kühl und ruhig, und es war eine Oase der Ruhe nach dem **Trubel auf** dem Markt. Alles wurde weggeräumt, und bald herrschte wieder die gewohnte Ruhe im Haus. Ich hatte alles, was ich brauchte, um **köstliche Mahlzeiten** für mich und meine Familie zuzubereiten. Es war schön, zu Hause zu sein.

dairy section.

The market was bustling with people, all of them eager to get their **hands** on the fresh produce and meat that were on offer. The air was thick with the smell of garlic and onions, and the sound of laughter and conversation filled the air. I made my way through the crowd, picking out the other items I needed for my weekly shop. I filled my **basket** with fruit and vegetables, pasta and bread, before heading to the checkout. The queue was long, but it moved quickly. Finally, the last of the **groceries** were bought, and it was time to go home. The car was loaded up, and the drive home was long and tedious. The traffic was heavy and the heat was oppressive. Finally, the car pulled into the driveway and the relief was palpable. The house was cool and quiet, and it was a haven after the **hustle** and bustle of the market. Everything was put away, and the house was soon back to its usual peace and quiet. I had everything I needed to make some **delicious** meals for myself and for my family. It was good to be home.

Verständnisfragen

1. Wohin geht die Person?

2. Was möchte die Person kaufen?

3. Wie viele Taschen hat die Person?

4. Wie weit ist der Markt entfernt?

5. Was macht die Person im Moment?

6. Was ist alles auf dem Markt?

7. Wie viele Personen befinden sich auf dem Markt?

8. Wie lange hat die Person gebraucht, um alles zu kaufen?

9. Wie ist die Person nach Hause gegangen?

10. Was hat die Person getan, als sie nach Hause kam?

Comprehension Questions

1. Where is the person going?

2. What does the person want to buy?

3. How many bags does the person have?

4. How far away is the market?

5. What is the person doing right now?

6. What is everything in the market?

7. How many people are in the market?

8. How long did it take the person to buy everything?

9. How did the person go home?

10. What did the person do when he or she got home?

In einem Cafe

Es war ein kühler Herbstmorgen, und ich hatte mich mit meiner Freundin Lily in unserem Lieblingscafé auf einen Kaffee verabredet. Ich wickelte mich warm in meinen Mantel und meinen Schal ein und machte mich auf den Weg. Die Blätter fielen von den Bäumen, und die Luft war etwas frisch, aber die Sonne schien, und es versprach, ein schöner Tag zu werden. Während ich ging, **dachte ich** darüber nach, wie gut es war, eine Freundin wie Lily zu haben. Wir waren seit Jahren befreundet, seit wir uns an der **Universität** kennen gelernt hatten. Uns verband die Liebe zum Kaffee und zum Plaudern in Cafés. Obwohl wir inzwischen in verschiedenen Stadtteilen wohnten, trafen wir uns immer noch einmal in der Woche auf einen Kaffee. Als ich im Café ankam, war Lily schon da und wartete auf mich. Wir umarmten uns zur Begrüßung und bestellten unsere Kaffees. Wir suchten uns einen Tisch am Fenster und setzten uns, um zu plaudern. Der **Kaffee** war wie immer köstlich, und es war so schön, sich mit Lily zu unterhalten. Wir sprachen über unsere Woche, unsere Jobs und unsere Pläne für die Zukunft. Es war immer so einfach, mit Lily zu reden, und ich hatte das Gefühl, dass ich ihr alles sagen konnte. Nach einer Weile wurden wir hungrig und **beschlossen,** etwas zu essen zu bestellen.

Wir **bestellten** unser Essen und suchten uns einen Platz am Fenster. Die Sonne schien durch das Fenster herein und verlieh allem eine warme und fröhliche Atmosphäre. Wir unterhielten uns, während wir

At a Cafe

It was a chilly **autumn** morning, and I had arranged to meet my friend Lily at our favourite cafe for a coffee. I wrapped up warm in my coat and scarf and set off. The leaves were falling from the trees and the air had a nip to it, but the sun was shining and it promised to be a beautiful day. As I walked, I **thought** about how good it was to have a friend like Lily. We had been friends for years, ever since we met at **university**. We bonded over our love of coffee and spending time chatting in cafes. Even though we now lived in different parts of the city, we still managed to meet up for coffee once a week. I arrived at the cafe, and Lily was already there, waiting for me. We hugged each other hello and then ordered our coffees. We found a table by the window and settled down to chat. The **coffee** was delicious, as always, and it was so nice to catch up with Lily. We talked about our week, our jobs, and our plans for the future. It was always so easy to talk to Lily, and I felt like I could tell her anything. After a while, we started to get hungry and **decided** to order some food.

We **ordered** our food and found a seat by the window. The sun was shining in through the window, making everything feel warm and happy. We chatted as we ate our food, enjoying the simple pleasure of being in each other's **company**. The cafe was busy, but it didn't feel crowded. There was a feeling of peace and contentment in the air. As we finished our food, we sat for a while longer, just enjoying the peaceful **atmosphere**. We talked for a while about different

aßen, und genossen das einfache Vergnügen, in der **Gesellschaft** des anderen zu sein. Das Café war gut besucht, aber es fühlte sich nicht überfüllt an. Es lag ein Gefühl von Frieden und Zufriedenheit in der Luft. Als wir mit dem Essen fertig waren, saßen wir noch eine Weile und genossen die friedliche **Atmosphäre**. Wir unterhielten uns noch eine Weile über verschiedene Dinge, die in unserem Leben passiert waren. Es war so schön, sich mit meiner Freundin auszutauschen und einfach **zu entspannen**. Die Sonne schien durch das Fenster, und wir hatten das Gefühl, dass **nichts** unseren perfekten Tag stören konnte.

Plötzlich hörte ich ein lautes Krachen. Ich drehte mich um und sah, dass ein Mann durch die Decke gefallen war und vor uns auf dem Boden lag. Er war mit Staub und Trümmern **bedeckt** und schien bewusstlos zu sein. Mein Freund und ich standen beide unter Schock und starrten auf den Mann, der auf dem Boden lag. Wir wussten nicht, was wir tun oder wen wir um Hilfe bitten sollten. Wir saßen einfach da und starrten ihn an, ohne zu wissen, was wir tun sollten. Nach ein paar Minuten riss ich mich zusammen und rief 911 an. Die Telefonistin sagte mir, dass bald jemand da sein würde. Ich legte den Hörer auf und erzählte meinem Freund, was die **Telefonistin** gesagt hatte. Wir saßen beide einfach da und warteten auf Hilfe. Es kam mir wie eine Ewigkeit vor, aber schließlich **tauchte** ein Krankenwagen auf. Die Sanitäter eilten herbei und begannen mit der Behandlung des Mannes. Sie stellten schnell fest, dass er verletzt war und in ein **Krankenhaus** gebracht werden musste.

things that had been going on in our lives. It was so nice to catch up with my friend and just **relax**. The sun was shining through the window, and it felt like **nothing** could ruin our perfect day.

Suddenly, I heard a loud crash. I turned around to see that a man had fallen through the ceiling and was lying on the floor in front of us. He was **covered** in dust and debris and appeared to be unconscious. My friend and I were both in shock as we stared at the man lying on the floor. We didn't know what to do or who to call for help. We just sat there staring at him, not knowing what to do. After a few minutes, I snapped out of it and called 911. The operator told me that someone would be there soon. I hung up the phone and told my friend what the **operator** had said. We both just sat there waiting for help to arrive. It felt like forever, but eventually an ambulance **showed** up. The paramedics rushed in and started working on the man. They quickly determined that he was injured and needed to be taken to the **hospital**.

Verständnisfragen

1. Woher kommt der Mann, der durch das Dach fällt?

2. Warum ist die Frau mit ihrer Freundin im Café?

3. Welches ist das Lieblingscafé der beiden Freunde?

4. Wie lange kennen sich die beiden Freunde schon?

5. Was ist das Lieblingsgetränk der beiden Freunde?

6. In welcher Stadt leben die beiden Freunde?

7. Wie oft treffen sich die beiden Freunde?

8. Worüber sprechen die beiden Freunde, als sie sich zum ersten Mal in ihrem Lieblingscafé treffen?

9. Was ist das Lieblingsessen der beiden Freunde?

10. Warum ist es so einfach, mit Lily zu sprechen?

Comprehension Questions

1. Where does the man who falls through the roof come from?

2. Why is the woman with her friend in the café?

3. What is the two friends' favorite café?

4. How long have the two friends known each other?

5. What is the two friends' favorite drink?

6. In which city do the two friends live?

7. How often do the two friends meet?

8. What do the two friends talk about when they first meet at their favorite café?

9. What is the favorite food of the two friends?

10. Why is it so easy to talk to Lily?

Schwimmen gehen

Der Pool war immer ein **erfrischender** Ort, und heute war es nicht anders. Die Sonne schien und das Wasser sah einladend aus. Ich holte tief Luft, tauchte ein und spürte die kühle Umarmung des Wassers. Ich schwamm eine Weile meine Runden, genoss die Bewegung und die Möglichkeit, den Kopf frei zu bekommen. Nach einer Weile stieg ich aus dem Wasser und trocknete mich ab, dann setzte ich mich auf ein Handtuch, um mich in der Sonne zu entspannen. Ich schloss die Augen und ließ die **Wärme** über mich ergehen, während sich meine Muskeln zu entspannen begannen. Plötzlich hörte ich ein Plätschern und öffnete die Augen, um meine kleine Schwester zu sehen, **die** im flachen Wasser herumplanschte. Ich lächelte und sah ihr eine Weile zu, dann stand ich auf und ging zu ihr hinüber. Wir unterhielten uns eine Weile, paddelten zusammen und genossen die Gesellschaft des anderen. Bald gesellten sich unsere Eltern zu uns, und wir verbrachten den Rest des Nachmittags mit Schwimmen und gemeinsamen Spielen. Es war immer schön, Zeit mit der Familie im Schwimmbad zu verbringen. **Der** Aufenthalt im Wasser scheint die Menschen zusammenzubringen. Vielleicht liegt es daran, dass wir alle gleich sind, wenn wir im Wasser sind - wir können unsere Schwächen nicht verstecken oder vorgeben, etwas zu sein, was wir nicht sind. Oder vielleicht liegt es einfach daran, dass es Spaß macht! **Was auch immer** der Grund ist, ich war einfach froh, dass wir alle zusammenkommen und die Gesellschaft

Going Swimming

The pool was always a **refreshing** place to be, and today was no different. The sun was shining and the water looked inviting. I took a deep breath and dove in, feeling the cool embrace of the water. I swam laps for a while, enjoying the exercise and the chance to clear my head. After a while, I got out and dried off, then sat down on a towel to relax in the sun. I closed my eyes and let the **warmth** wash over me, feeling my muscles start to relax. Suddenly, I heard a splash and opened my eyes to see my little sister **paddling** around in the shallow end. I smiled and watched her for a while, then stood up and walked over to her. We chatted for a bit and paddled around together, enjoying each other's company. Soon, our parents joined us, and we spent the rest of the afternoon swimming and playing games together. It was always so nice to spend time with the family at the pool. There's **something** about being in the water that just seems to bring people together. Maybe it's because we're all equal when we're in the water—we can't hide our flaws or pretend to be something we're not. Or maybe it's just because it's fun! **Whatever** the reason, I was just glad that we could all come together and enjoy each other's company in such a special place.

The sun was beating down on my skin and the smell of chlorine was in the air. I could hear the sounds of kids laughing and splashing around in the pool. I was lying on a **lounge** chair next to the pool, soaking up the sun and **enjoying** the day. I had my eyes closed and was

des anderen an einem so besonderen Ort genießen konnten.

Die Sonne brannte auf meine Haut und der Geruch von Chlor lag in der Luft. Ich hörte das Lachen der Kinder, die im Pool planschten. Ich lag auf einem Liegestuhl neben dem Pool, genoss die Sonne und **den** Tag. Ich hatte meine Augen geschlossen und wollte gerade einschlafen, als ich hörte, wie jemand auf mich zukam. Ich öffnete meine Augen und sah eine Frau neben mir stehen. Sie trug einen Bikini und hatte sich ein Handtuch um die Taille geschlungen. Sie hatte langes blondes Haar und blaue Augen. In der Hand hielt sie ein Fläschchen mit **Sonnenschutzmittel**. "Stört es Sie, wenn ich Ihnen den Rücken mit Sonnencreme einschmiere?", fragte sie. "Nein, das ist in Ordnung", sagte ich und setzte mich auf, damit sie meinen Rücken erreichen konnte. Ich spürte ihre Hände auf meiner Haut, als sie die Sonnencreme auftrug.

Ihre Berührung war sanft, und der Duft der Sonnencreme war beruhigend. Ich schloss wieder die Augen und ließ mich entspannen. Ich konnte hören, **wie** sie sich bewegte, aber ich öffnete meine Augen nicht. Ich war damit zufrieden, einfach nur in der Sonne zu liegen und dem Rauschen der Wellen zu lauschen, die an den Strand **schlugen**. Nach ein paar Minuten ging sie weg, und ich öffnete die Augen. Ich sah ihr nach, wie sie zu ihrem Liegestuhl zurückging und ihr Buch in die Hand nahm. Sie ließ sich in ihrem Sessel nieder und begann zu lesen.

just about to drift off to sleep when I heard someone walking up to me. I opened my eyes and saw a woman standing next to me. She was wearing a bikini and had a towel wrapped around her waist. She had long blonde hair and blue eyes. She was holding a bottle of **sunscreen** in her hand. "Do you mind if I put some sunscreen on your back?" she asked. "No, that's fine," I said, sitting up so she could reach my back. I felt her hands on my skin as she applied the sunscreen.

Her touch was gentle and the scent of the sunscreen was soothing. I closed my eyes again and let myself relax. I could hear the **sound** of her moving around, but I didn't open my eyes. I was content just lying there in the sun, listening to the sound of the waves **crashing** against the shore. After a few minutes, she walked away, and I opened my eyes. I watched her as she walked back to her lounge chair and picked up her book. She settled into her chair and began reading. I closed my eyes again and let myself drift off to sleep.

Verständnisfragen

1. Wo war der Erzähler, als er die Geschichte begann?

2. Was riecht der Erzähler, wenn er seine Augen öffnet?

3. Was hört der Erzähler, als er seine Augen öffnet?

4. Wem gehört die Sonnencreme, die die Frau dem Erzähler gibt?

5. Wovon träumt der Erzähler?

6. Warum ist das Schwimmen im Meer für den Erzähler so besonders?

7 Wie fühlt sich das Wasser an, in dem der Erzähler schwimmt?

8. Was sieht der Erzähler, als er aus dem Wasser kommt?

9. Was tut die Frau, nachdem sie den Erzähler mit Sonnencreme eingecremt hat?

Comprehension Questions

1. Where was the narrator when the story begins?

2. What does the narrator smell when he opens his eyes?

3. What does the narrator hear when he opens his eyes?

4. Whose sunscreen does the woman give the narrator?

5. What does the narrator dream about?

6. Why is swimming in the ocean so special to the narrator?

7. What does the water feel like when the narrator swims in it?

8. What does the narrator see when he comes out of the water?

9. What does the woman do after she has applied sun cream to the narrator?

Mähen des Rasens

Es ist 10 Uhr morgens an einem **Sommersamstag**, und die Sonne brennt bereits erbarmungslos auf die Erde. Sie stapfen in die Garage, um den Rasenmäher zu holen, und haben das Gefühl, dass Sie zu harter Arbeit **verurteilt werden**. Du fängst an, den Rasen zu mähen, wobei du darauf achtest, dass du schön langsam vorgehst, damit du keine Stelle übersiehst. Während du mähst, denkst du daran, wie gut es sich anfühlt, draußen an der frischen Luft zu sein. Als du den Rasenmäher hin und her schiebst, siehst du aus dem **Augenwinkel** deinen Nachbarn. Sie winken und grüßen, und er winkt zurück.

Nach ein paar Minuten sind Sie fertig und gehen zum Haus Ihres Nachbarn, um mit ihm im Vorgarten ein Bier zu trinken. Es ist ein **perfekter** Tag - nicht zu heiß, und es weht eine leichte Brise. Sie sitzen im Schatten des Baumes, nippen an Ihrem Bier und unterhalten sich mit Ihrem Nachbarn. Es sind Tage wie dieser, an denen man den Sommer zu schätzen weiß. Dann **gehen Sie** ins Haus, um ein wohlverdientes Bier zu trinken. Sie lassen sich in einen Stuhl auf der Veranda fallen, öffnen die Dose und lassen einen zufriedenen Seufzer los. Das Geräusch des Rasenmähers tritt in den Hintergrund, während du dich im Schatten entspannst und die **Ruhe** des Augenblicks genießt. Das Bier schmeckt besonders gut nach all der harten Arbeit in der Hitze. Ich wollte gerade ins Haus gehen, als ich nebenan ein Geräusch hörte.

Mowing the Lawn

It's 10 in the morning on a summer **Saturday**, and the sun is already beating down mercilessly. You trudge out to the garage to fetch the lawn mower, feeling like you're being **sentenced** to hard labor. You start mowing the lawn, making sure to go nice and slow so you don't miss any spots. As you're mowing, you think about how good it feels to be outside in the fresh air. As you start pushing the mower back and forth across the lawn, you see your neighbour out of the corner of your **eye**. You wave and say hi, and he waves back.

After a few minutes, you're done, and you head over to your neighbour's house to have a beer with him in the front garden. It's a **perfect** day—not too hot, with a gentle breeze blowing. You sit there in the shade of the tree, sipping your beer and chatting with your neighbour. It's days like this that make you appreciate summertime. Then you **head** inside for a well-deserved beer. You flop down in a chair on the front porch and crack open the can, letting out a contented sigh. The sound of the mower fades into the background as you relax in the shade, enjoying the **peacefulness** of the moment. The beer tastes extra good after all that hard work in the heat. I was about to head inside when I heard a noise next door.

It **sounded** like someone was crying. I stopped mowing and walked over to the fence that separated our yards. I peered over and saw my neighbor, Mrs. Johnson, crying on her porch swing. I called out to her, but she

Es **hörte sich an**, als ob jemand weinen würde. Ich hörte auf zu mähen und ging zu dem Zaun, der unsere Gärten trennte. Ich spähte hinüber und sah meine Nachbarin, Mrs. Johnson, weinend auf ihrer Verandaschaukel. Ich rief nach ihr, aber sie hörte mich nicht. Ich kletterte über den Zaun und ging zu ihr hinüber. "Mrs. Johnson, geht es Ihnen gut?" fragte ich. Sie schaute mich mit Tränen in den Augen an und schüttelte den Kopf. "Nein, mir geht es nicht gut", sagte sie. "Meine Katze ist gestern gestorben." Ich war schockiert. Ich wußte nicht, was ich sagen sollte. Ich stand nur unbeholfen da und wusste nicht, was ich tun sollte. Schließlich legte ich ihr die Hand auf die **Schulter** und sagte: "Es tut mir so leid, Mrs. Johnson. Wenn ich Ihnen irgendwie helfen kann, lassen Sie es mich bitte wissen. "Sie schüttelte den Kopf und sagte: "Nein, es gibt **nichts**, was man tun könnte." Dann stand sie auf und ging in ihr Haus. Ich stand einen Moment lang da und wusste nicht, was ich tun sollte. Dann mähte ich wieder meinen Rasen. Als ich fertig war, musste ich unweigerlich an Frau Johnson und ihre Katze denken.

didn't hear me. I climbed over the fence and walked over to her. "Mrs. Johnson, are you okay?" I asked. She looked up at me with tears in her eyes and shook her head. "No, I'm not okay," she said. "My cat died yesterday." I was shocked. I didn't know what to say. I just stood there awkwardly, not knowing what to do. Finally, I put my hand on her **shoulder** and said, "I'm so sorry, Mrs. Johnson. If there's anything I can do to help, please let me know. " She shook her head and said, "No, there's **nothing** anyone can do." Then she got up and went inside her house. I stood there for a moment, not knowing what to do. Then I went back to mowing my lawn. As I finished up, I couldn't help but think about Mrs. Johnson and her cat.

Verständnisfragen

1. Wie spät ist es?

2. Wo mäht die Person?

3. Wie fühlt sich die Person?

4. Warum muss die Person langsam mähen?

5. Was für ein Wetter ist es?

6. Was macht die Person nach dem Mähen?

7. Was hört die Person, bevor sie nach Hause geht?

8. Wer ist bei Mrs. Johnson?

9. Warum weint Mrs. Johnson?

10. Was sagt die Person zu Frau Johnson?

Comprehension Questions

1. What time is it?

2. Where is the person mowing?

3. How does the person feel?

4. Why does the person have to mow slowly?

5. What kind of weather is it?

6. What is the person doing after mowing?

7. What does the person hear before going home?

8. Who is with Mrs. Johnson?

9. Why is Mrs. Johnson crying?

10. What does the person say to Mrs. Johnson?

Zum Haareschneiden

Ich wollte mir schon seit Wochen die Haare schneiden lassen, aber irgendwie habe ich es immer wieder aufgeschoben. Aber da **Weihnachten** vor der Tür stand, wusste ich, dass ich es nicht länger aufschieben konnte. Ich wollte beim Weihnachtsessen meiner Familie nicht wie ein schmuddeliges Etwas erscheinen. Also machte ich mich am frühen Weihnachtsmorgen auf den Weg zum Friseur. Obwohl es noch früh war, war der Salon schon voll mit anderen Leuten, **die sich** für die Feiertage die Haare machen ließen. Ich nahm meinen Platz in der Schlange ein und wartete, bis ich an der Reihe war. Endlich war ich mit dem Stuhl dran. Die Friseurin, eine freundliche Frau namens Jill, fragte mich, was ich wollte. "Nur einen Trimmschnitt, nichts allzu Drastisches", antwortete ich. Jill machte sich an die Arbeit und schnippelte an meinem Haar herum. Während sie arbeitete, begann ich mich zu entspannen. Es war ein gutes Gefühl, mich endlich um mich selbst zu kümmern. In letzter Zeit war ich so sehr damit beschäftigt gewesen, mich um alle anderen zu kümmern, dass ich meine eigenen Bedürfnisse vernachlässigt hatte. Aber das war **vorbei**. Von nun an wollte ich mir Zeit für mich nehmen.

Als Jill fertig war, schaute ich in den Spiegel und war mit dem, was ich sah, zufrieden. Mein Haar sah ordentlich und glänzend aus - perfekt für Festtagsfeiern. Ich **bedankte mich bei** Jill und nahm **mir vor, öfter**

Getting a Haircut

I had been meaning to get a haircut for weeks, but somehow always managed to put it off. But with **Christmas** just around the corner, I knew I couldn't put it off any longer. I didn't want to show up to my family's Christmas dinner looking like a scruffy mess. So, early on Christmas morning, I made my way to the salon. Even though it was early, the salon was already busy with other people **getting** their hair done for the holiday. I took my place in the line and waited my turn. Finally, it was my turn in the chair. The stylist, a friendly woman named Jill, asked me what I wanted. "Just a trim, nothing too drastic," I replied. Jill got to work, snipping away at my hair. As she worked, I began to relax. It felt good to finally be taking care of myself. I had been so busy lately, running around taking care of everyone else, that I had let my own needs fall by the wayside. But not **anymore**. From now on, I was going to make time for myself.

When Jill was finished, I looked in the mirror and was pleased with what I saw. My hair looked tidy and polished—perfect for holiday gatherings. I **thanked** Jill and made a **mental** note to come back more often. From now on, I will take care of myself first and foremost. She got to work snipping away at my hair. I thought about how thankful I was that I had finally gotten around to getting my haircut. It felt good to know that I would look presentable for Christmas **dinner**. No longer would I have to worry about my family teasing me about my "scruffy" appearance. After a few minutes,

wiederzukommen. Von nun an werde ich mich in erster Linie um mich selbst kümmern. Sie machte sich an die Arbeit und schnippelte an meinem Haar herum. Ich dachte darüber nach, wie dankbar ich war, dass ich endlich dazu gekommen war, mir die Haare schneiden zu lassen. Es war ein gutes Gefühl zu wissen, dass ich zum **Weihnachtsessen** vorzeigbar aussehen würde. Ich musste mir keine Sorgen mehr machen, dass meine Familie mich wegen meines "ungepflegten" Aussehens hänseln würde. Nach ein paar Minuten war der Friseur mit dem Schneiden meiner Haare fertig und föhnte sie kurz. Ich schaute in den Spiegel und war zufrieden mit dem, was ich sah - ein gepflegtes Aussehen, das perfekt für das Weihnachtsessen sein würde. Jetzt, da mein Haarschnitt erledigt war, konnte ich mich darauf konzentrieren, die Feiertage mit meiner Familie zu genießen. Und dafür war ich umso dankbarer.

Es fühlte sich so **befreiend an**, und ich war begeistert, wie mein neuer Haarschnitt aussah. Nachdem ich meinen Haarschnitt bezahlt hatte, ging ich nach Hause und fing an, für meine Reise zu packen. Ich **konnte es kaum** erwarten, meiner Familie und meinen Freunden meinen neuen Look zu zeigen. Ich wusste, dass sie überrascht sein würden, wenn sie mich sahen. Am Tag meines Fluges kam ich rechtzeitig am Flughafen an. Ich passierte die Sicherheitskontrolle ohne Probleme und war bald auf dem Weg. Als ich an meinem Zielort ankam, konnte ich die Aufregung in der Luft spüren. Weihnachten lag definitiv in der Luft! Meine Familie war da, um mich am Flughafen zu begrüßen, und sie waren alle begeistert von meinem neuen Haarschnitt.

the stylist was finished trimming my hair and gave me a quick blow dry. I looked in the mirror and was happy with what I saw—a clean-cut look that would be perfect for Christmas dinner. Now that my haircut was out of the way, I could focus on enjoying the holiday with my family. And I was even more thankful for that.

It felt so **liberating**, and I loved the way my new haircut looked. After I paid for my haircut, I went home and started packing for my trip. I **couldn't** wait to show off my new look to my family and friends. I knew they would be surprised when they saw me. On the day of my flight, I arrived at the airport with plenty of time to spare. I went through security without any problems, and soon I was on my way. As soon as I arrived at my destination, I could feel the excitement in the air. Christmas was definitely in the air! My family was there to greet me at the airport, and they were all amazed at my new haircut.

Verständnisfragen

1. Was musste der Protagonist vor Weihnachten tun?

2. Wie hat sich die Protagonistin gefühlt, als sie für sich selbst sorgte?

3. Wer hat dem Protagonisten die Haare gestutzt?

4. Warum wollte die Familie der Protagonistin sie hänseln?

5. Wie hat sich die Protagonistin gefühlt, nachdem sie ihren Haarschnitt bekommen hat?

6. Was hat die Protagonistin getan, nachdem sie sich die Haare schneiden ließ?

7. Wie hat die Familie der Protagonistin auf ihren Haarschnitt reagiert?

8. Was hat der Protagonist an Heiligabend gemacht?

9. Was hat die Erfahrung des Protagonisten zu etwas Besonderem gemacht?

Comprehension Questions

1. What did the protagonist need to do before Christmas?

2. How did the protagonist feel about taking care of herself?

3. Who trimmed the protagonist's hair?

4. Why was the protagonist's family going to tease her?

5. How did the protagonist feel after getting her haircut?

6. What did the protagonist do after getting her haircut?

7. What was the protagonist's family's reaction to her haircut?

8. What did the protagonist do on Christmas Eve?

9. What made the protagonist's experience more special?

Der Park

Die Sonne ging gerade unter, und der Park war leer. Ich saß auf der Bank und wartete auf meine **Freundin**. Wir hatten uns vor einer Stunde hier verabredet, aber sie war immer zu spät. Gerade als ich aufgeben und nach Hause gehen wollte, sah ich sie auf mich zulaufen.

"Es tut mir so leid", keuchte sie, als sie die Bank erreichte. "Mein Zug **hatte Verspätung**."

"Ist schon gut", sagte ich **verzeihend**. "Ich bin auch gerade erst gekommen."

Wir setzten uns hin und unterhielten uns eine Weile, wobei wir uns über das Leben des jeweils anderen unterhielten, seit wir uns das letzte Mal gesehen hatten. Die Unterhaltung verlief **mühelos**, und es kam uns vor, als sei seit unserer letzten Begegnung überhaupt keine Zeit vergangen. Als die Sonne unterging, verabschiedeten wir uns und gingen unsere eigenen Wege. Das nächste Mal, als wir uns trafen, war es in einem anderen Park. Wieder war sie spät dran, aber das machte mir nichts aus. Es war schön, jemanden zum Reden zu haben, der mich **verstand**. Wir sprachen über unsere Träume und **Hoffnungen**, über die Dinge, die wir in unserem Leben tun wollten. Sie erzählte mir von ihren Plänen, die Welt zu bereisen, und ich erzählte von meinem Traum, Schriftstellerin zu werden. Als die Sonne an einem anderen Tag unterging, verabschiedeten wir uns noch einmal und versprachen uns, diesmal in Kontakt zu bleiben.

Die Jahre vergingen, und unsere **Freundschaft** blieb

The Park

The sun was setting, and the park was empty. I sat on the bench, waiting for my **friend**. We had planned to meet here an hour ago, but she was always late. Just as I was about to give up and go home, I saw her running towards me.

"I'm so sorry," she panted as she reached the bench. "My train was **delayed**."

"It's okay," I said **forgivingly**. "I just got here myself."

We sat down and chatted for a while, catching up on each other's lives since we last met. The conversation flowed **easily**, and it felt like no time had passed at all since we last saw each other. As the sun set, we said our goodbyes and went our separate ways. The next time we met, it was in a different park. Again, she was late, but I didn't mind. It was nice to have someone to talk to who **understood** me. We talked about our dreams and **aspirations**, things we wanted to do with our lives. She told me about her plans to travel the world, and I shared my dream of becoming a writer. As the sun set on another day, we said goodbye once again, promising to keep in touch this time.

Years passed, and our **friendship** remained strong even though we lived in different parts of the country now. We kept in touch through letters and occasional phone calls, sharing news of our lives with each other. When she announced that she was getting married, I wasn't **surprised** - she had always been the **adventurous** type. But when she asked me if I would

bestehen, obwohl wir jetzt in verschiedenen Teilen des Landes lebten. Wir hielten den Kontakt durch Briefe und gelegentliche Telefonate aufrecht und teilten uns gegenseitig die Neuigkeiten aus unserem Leben mit. Als sie ankündigte, dass sie heiraten würde, war ich nicht **überrascht** - sie war schon immer der **abenteuerlustige** Typ gewesen. Aber als sie mich fragte, ob ich ihre Trauzeugin bei ihrer Hochzeitsfeier sein würde, die am anderen Ende der Welt stattfand, musste ich sie erst einmal überzeugen! Letztendlich konnte ich jedoch nicht zulassen, dass meine beste Freundin ohne mich an ihrer Seite heiratet, und so **stimmte** ich trotz meiner Befürchtungen (und nach langem Bitten ihrerseits!) zu, das **Abenteuer** meines Lebens mitzumachen.

Endlich war der Tag der **Hochzeit** gekommen. Ich war nervös, aber auch aufgeregt, bei einem so wichtigen Moment im Leben meiner Freundin dabei zu sein. Die Zeremonie war wunderschön, und sie sah glücklich aus, als sie ihr Gelübde ablegte. **Danach** feierten wir mit einer großen Party - es schien, als ob jeder, den sie kannte, gekommen war, um mit ihr zu feiern! Es war ein **magischer** Tag, den ich nie vergessen werde, und unsere Freundschaft ist nach diesem Abenteuer nur noch stärker geworden. Heute, Jahre später, halten wir immer noch Kontakt. Wir haben uns beide sehr verändert, seit wir uns kennengelernt haben, aber unsere Freundschaft ist so stark wie eh und je. Wann immer wir uns treffen - sei es in einem Park oder am **anderen Ende der** Welt - fühlt es sich an, als wäre keine Zeit vergangen.

be her maid of honor at her wedding ceremony taking place halfway around the world from where I lived... that took some convincing! In the end though I couldn't let my best friend get married without me by her side so despite my fears (and after much pleading from her!)I **agreed** to go along for what turned out to be the **adventure** of a lifetime.

The day of the **wedding** finally arrived. I was nervous, but excited to be a part of such an important moment in my friend's life. The ceremony was beautiful, and she looked happy as she said her vows. **Afterward**, we celebrated with a big party – it seemed like everyone she knew had come to celebrate with her! It was a **magical** day that will never forget, and our friendship only grew stronger after that adventure. Now, years later, we still keep in touch. We've both **changed** a lot since we first met, but our friendship is as strong as ever. Whenever we meet up - whether it's in a park or **halfway** around the world - it feels like no time has passed at all.

Verständnisfragen

1. Wo haben sich die Autorin und ihr Freund zum ersten Mal getroffen?

2. Warum kam der Freund des Autors zu spät zu ihrem Treffen?

3. Worüber sprachen die Freunde, als sie sich Jahre später wieder trafen?

4. Wie hat sich die Autorin gefühlt, als sie an der Hochzeit ihrer Freundin teilnahm?

5. Beschreiben Sie den Rahmen der Hochzeitszeremonie.

6. Wie hat sich die Freundschaft zwischen den beiden Frauen im Laufe der Zeit verändert?

7. Was ist der Traum des Autors?

8. Wohin plant der Freund des Autors zu reisen?

9. Warum hat die Autorin gezögert, an der Hochzeit ihrer Freundin teilzunehmen?

Comprehension Questions

1. Where did the author and her friend first meet?

2. Why was the author's friend late to their meeting?

3. What did the friends talk about when they met up again years later?

4. How did the author feel about attending her friend's wedding ceremony?

5. Describe the setting of the wedding ceremony.

6. How has the friendship between the two women changed over time?

7. What is the author's dream?

8. Where does the author's friend plan to travel?

9. Why was the author hesitant to attend her friend's wedding ceremony?

www.ingramcontent.com/pod-product-compliance
Lightning Source LLC
Chambersburg PA
CBHW061535120726
48001CB00004B/1562